from METAPHYSICAL *to* MYSTICAL

A Study of the Way

by
Dorothy Elder

This paperback edition published by

Doriel Publishing Company
Dorothy Elder
2557 South Dover, #75
Denver, Colorado 80227

ISBN   0-9631673-0-8

Library of Congress Data
9   1   9   0   7   3   1

First Edition

Also by Dorothy Elder

Revelation: For A New Age
(The Book of Revelation)

Women of the Bible Speak to Women of Today

The Song of Songs and Enlightenment

Heaven is Here
(A Collection of Poetry)

Dedicated to

MYSTICS OF ALL AGES

CONTENTS

PREFACE

Joseph Campbell, the popular mythologist and religionist, said in the TV series "Transformation of Myth Through Time" (PBS 1989) that our society has become totally secularized in government, economics, education, and religion. We do not have a myth, a religion, he said, by which to live. Spiritual principles, for the most part, are being totally disregarded. The religious life is ethical, not mystical, and people are seeking for an answer to the crime, to the anti-culture, to the drug problems, etc. He said that people are hunting for the mystical experience, consciously or unconsciously, but do not know where to look.

Anyone who has seriously observed the human condition, especially in the United States of America, knows this is true. Many are searching for some meaning in life beyond the materialistic realm with which they are surrounded.

I believe that we each have a deep need to reunite with the All. Our soul is hungry to come Home. We have been There before. We all long to return. It is said that all of us are potential Mystics, and until one awakens to that direction they will be dissatisfied. I happen to believe that it is that Inner Guide, Universal Energy, God, that pervades everything which is calling to each one. The search will continue and one may feel fragmented until the answer is found.

My goal, in this writing, is to help those who are searching, seriously, to find an answer either on the metaphysical Path or the mystical Path. The metaphysical and the mystical have much in common. One blends into the other. But there are differences. Just as the metaphysical philosophy has satisfied the Spiritual needs of many, so the Mystical Path can satisfy at a higher, deeper level. The metaphysical can lead to the mystical.

I believe the next evolutionary stage for humanity is the recognition of the Cosmic Christ here and now. Carrying this to its complete realization is the Mystic Way.

The strength of the rise of interest in mysticism is supported by or may be led by the rise of the divine feminine in the consciousness of both men and women on this planet. Mysticism is basically intuitive living, Guidance from the Inner Christ, and balanced by the intellect. Intuition is a feminine characteristic. Thus the two, mysticism and the rise of the divine feminine, feed each other.

The masculine, it would appear, is becoming weary in the efforts to solve the problems of the world, in leading human beings to a higher consciousness. We are realizing that the masculine (intellect) needs the feminine (intuition) for balance.

Evidence of the growing interest in mysticism is demonstrated by the classes on the subject offered in many churches. The proliferation of books on mysticism also underscores this rise in interest.

Mysticism is a balance of masculine and feminine. Maybe that is why the patriarchal religions have not encouraged it in their adherents. To be led by the Inner Spirit instead of the church authorities is a big jump for many but is coming whether or not the churches are ready. Many have left traditional religious institutions, both Jewish and Christian. I believe they are hearing the call from Within.

Another factor that is moving us toward the mystical Way is the attention that humankind is giving to Mother Earth. Realization that our lives depend on the bounty of Mother Earth, and the concern with our damaging of the environment, has given rise to interest in the feminine. We have ignored too long the feminine and the mystical. The flame has not died through the Ages. It has ever been alive in the hearts, the souls, of many. Now it is bearing fruition.

As I see it, the metaphysical Way is the mystical Way but at a different level. The metaphysical has much of the same direction as the mystical Way. (Metaphysical means reliance on something beyond the physical sense.) Many are satisfied with the metaphysical Way of life, the philosophy taught, and have no desire to continue on the mystical Way. The mystical choice is frightening to some for it seems so individual, indeed lonely. The Mystic, however, claims that they are never lonely for Oneness with God is a "crowd." The 21st century will bring us greater freedom to follow this choice if we so desire.

I would also hope that this discussion of the metaphysical spiritual philosophy would encourage the reader to choose this Way that could bring them a greater measure of peace, in their inner as well as outer life. The explanation of the metaphysical might also encourage those who are looking for something in the spiritual realm to bring more balance to their secular life, to choose that Way.

The mystical Way has not always been entitled religious. The term religion commonly implies the worship of an outer God or god. The mystical Way emphasizes the worship of an Inner Knowing, a following of an Inner Spirit that resides in all and is part of or is God. Although the metaphysician may be tuned in to that Center through prayer and meditation, they often use conscious thought to bring their good to them. The Mystic knows that their Good is already there and that God will provide the Way to reach It through spiritual means. The Mystic allows the Spirit, a part of the unconscious, to *lead* their thoughts.

Jesus the Christ taught, healed, overcame death all from his Father, his Inner Spirit (John 14:10). There have been many sects that have emphasized Inner Guidance also. It is a commonality among all major religions. We shall discuss other Mystics and their following of the Illuminative Light, the Inner Voice, and how they took this Spiritual Knowing to others through service to God and humankind.

It is thought by many that the time is now for us to turn from ethical religion to mystical religion. The Cosmic Christ is moving in hearts and lives all over this planet. Matthew Fox, in his book *The Coming of the Cosmic Christ*, sees this movement as already here. Many are ready for it. The movement toward freedom of choice in many countries attests to this need. I hope that something I have written strikes a bell of Truth in your heart and mind, and if you are ready, the metaphysical or the mystical will become the Way chosen. All that is needed is an openness of heart and mind to the possibility and a commitment to finding the Wholeness that we all seek.

In this treatise I have confined my description of the metaphysical philosophy to the three major divisions of the metaphysical movement: Unity, Science of Mind/Religious Science, and Divine Science. There are many more branches with very similar teachings not included.

The Mystic Path seems to be chosen for us rather than our choosing It. This can also be true of the metaphysical Path. We are here for a Purpose and it unfolds gradually as we open our Self to It. Most biblical references are from the New International Version if not otherwise noted.

PART I

Chapter 1

WHAT'S THE DIFFERENCE?

I have thought for a long time that the mystical is possibly the basis of the metaphysical movement. However, most adherents of the metaphysical movement have not thought of themselves as Mystics. If they have it has been as potential Mystics. It is a scary idea for many, for our society has not encouraged us to be mystical. It has encouraged us to be active, involved, one with the world, and more intellectual than spiritual. And mysticism? It has been thought to encourage quiet, solitude, withdrawal from attachment to the world and materialism, chastity vows and total dependence on God—not on the government, the intellect, or Social Security. Who would choose that route? Only an eccentric and may Heaven forbid, no one wants to be so considered!

But when we look to the foundation of metaphysical we see similar teachings such as prayer and meditation; going Within for Guidance; affirming the positive and the beautiful in our life; depending on Spirit to take care of our needs; pointing toward a final goal of Perfection in our earth living. All of these and others are the foundation of metaphysical philosophy. And these are mystical, also.

I have been (in this lifetime) in the metaphysical movement for over 20 years. Formerly, I believe, I was there for many lifetimes. I knew, before I ever studied a metaphysical text, that all was Good; that sickness was caused by thought and probably could be cured by thought and prayer; that all were forgiven and loved by God, whatever their error; that Joy came from the Lord, etc. As I have attended New Thought churches, read hundreds of books, studied in classes and seminars, written five books, taught in metaphysical centers, I have seen and experienced the growth in Consciousness of many, many people. But I have seen them come and go.

Some come to these founts of learning for a period and leave for various reasons. Some leave and return. Some find the teaching is not for them in their present life. Some find the freedom of choice too overwhelming and return to their traditional church. And some leave because the teaching is too hard to understand.

But some leave because they have learned all the principles taught and have applied them in their life. They have prosperity, loving relationships, health, and inspiration, but say: "Now what?" "Where do I go from here?" "What more is there?" They know there is more, for our Soul is never at peace completely until it finds Its home with All That Is. And so they leave the church or center. Their life is so, so much better but there is still a feeling of unfulfillment. This book is for those sensitive Souls who are wanting more and who may be within or without the metaphysical or New Thought movement, terms that can be read interchangeably.

Mysticism is as old as the human race. There have always been those who saw beyond the sight of the two eyes; beyond the physical, who seemed to have some secret that the masses were not able to fathom or had no interest in. The mystical has been demonstrated and written about in the Hindu literature (the Vedas); the Buddhist literature (the Sutras); the Taoist (Tao te Ching); the Muslim (the Koran); and in our Holy Bible. But the Protestant Christian church has not made it a major teaching. The Catholic church permitted orison, or meditation, among the monks and nuns in the monastery but the masses knew little about it. This has changed now as meditation, the basis of mysticism, has swept into our Western culture.

The Christian church, in the past, has often declared heretical the individual who may have turned toward Inner Autonomy. It has emphasized the need for the church structure and the leader's guidance in order to help the individual tolerate and overcome this world of sin and pain. As a result, mysticism has gone underground.

2

During the past centuries various groups have practiced the Presence through meditation, sometimes under the guise of trying to turn metals into gold, as the Alchemists did. The Gnostics flourished for a while until they became a threat to the Church. There were other teachings that encouraged it: Rosicrucians, Hasidics, Swedenborgians, Theosophists, etc. All encouraged meditation, but many of them had their strict rules which members must follow in order to be in good standing. When religion has been organized it has tended to become autocratic in order to perpetuate the organization.

When the Transcendentalists, in America, opened up the minds of philosophically directed Americans to the idea of transcending this physical world by direct attention to the Inner Self, a transformation started. Among these Transcendentalists were Ralph Waldo Emerson, Amos Bronson Alcott (father of Louisa May Alcott), Theodore Parker, Henry David Thoreau and others. They gave heed to their own Inner Guidance. From these teachers and also from the teachings of Phinias Quimby the metaphysical movement arose, or perhaps they arose together. Its *Time* had come. Mary Baker Eddy established the Christian Science philosophy which also impacted the metaphysical teaching.

An excellent history of the metaphysical movement may be found in *Spirits in Rebellion* by Charles Braden. If you are further interested in studying some of the teachings of the leaders and founders, you may want to read some of their writings:

New Testament: Jesus Christ's teachings in the Four Gospels of Matthew, Mark, Luke, and John

Mary Baker Eddy: *Science and Health*

Emma Curtis Hopkins: *Scientific Christian Mental Practice* and *High Mysticism*

Charles Fillmore: *Twelve Powers of Man*

Emilie Cady: *Lessons in Truth*

Ernest Holmes: *The Science of Mind*

Divine Science: Its Principles and Practice (From writings by Fannie James and Malinda Cramer)

Emmet Fox: *The Sermon on the Mount*

3

Mystics have come out of the Christian Church teaching. There are some who have been declared saints by the Catholic Church. It is not clear, however, that all saints were Mystics. Some of the mystic Saints are: St.Augustine of Hippo; St.Bernard of Clairvoux; St. Julian of Norwich; St.Catherine of Siena; St.Teresa of Avila; St. John of the Cross. (See *Silent Fire* by Capps and Wright for additional information on Mystics.)

There are those who consider some later-day Mystics as being genuine: Pierre Teilhard de Chardin; Thomas Merton; Walt Whitman; William Blake; Ralph Waldo Emerson; Henry David Thoreau; Sri Aurobindo; Evelyn Underhill; Richard Bucke; and others.

Now out of the metaphysical movement we have a few that are considered Mystics by those who write about them. Emmet Fox is undeniably entitled to be so designated. Many place Charles Fillmore, Malinda Cramer, Nona Brooks, Ernest Holmes, and Emma Curtis Hopkins there also, all founders of metaphysical movements.

Who is a Mystic is dependent upon our definition of the term. And so let us try to briefly define the metaphysical and the mystical. Fuller definitions will be found in chapters headed either metaphysical or mystical.

The New Thought approach has many qualities in common with mysticism. The metaphysical, however, deals more with going beyond the physical. It is centered upon Divine ideas, of God within all, but it stresses *the use* of the God Presence more than allowing the God Presence *to use* the mind, body, spirit of the person as in mysticism. It teaches the potential for wholeness, of Oneness with God. It stresses the Christ within, the Spirit within each and teaches that God is Omnipresent and that Good is the only Power in the Universe. This Presence within makes each one a co-creator with God and one's special gifts can come forth. Metaphysics teaches a process. At first the process seeks adjustment to the world, success in the world, comfort and health of the body. It involves seeing only the positive in everything. These are some of the more popular practices and results of the metaphysical teaching.

Joseph Campbell in a TV series "Transformation of Myth Through Time" (PBS 1989) said that the majority of humankind is centered in what he has designated as the three lower chakras. These, he says, are health, wealth, and progeny. There are many in the metaphysical movement who come to it because of dissatisfaction with all or one of these needs. The desire for progeny may be translated into the need for meaningful relationships. And many get their needs fulfilled. However, Campbell also said that when one reaches the fourth chakra, the heart or love chakra, then a fuller meaning of love comes forth and serving others becomes most important. Thus the mystical Path may be entered at that level.

In the metaphysical, much emphasis is given to thought. The conscious, unconscious, and superconscious are three divisions given the intellect. Thoughts carried in any of these three bring experiences into the life of the practitioner. When the conscious mind is centered on the Good and not on the negative, then only Good accrues in one's life. However, the need to clear the unconscious and the conscious of negativities may be necessary before the positive thoughts will be fully effective, a process called denial in New Thought teachings. Thus emphasis is given to getting rid of negative thinking through denial, followed by affirmation. Thought of the positive is very important in the beginning of the practice of the metaphysical Way as it is throughout the experience. In the mystical stance one goes beyond thinking to intuition which defined is guidance from the Higher Self. The thoughts are stopped and the intuition is the basis for the thoughts.

The line is fine between metaphysical and mystical. The following is an attempt to define the mystical.

The main quality of mysticism is the letting go of all human desires and letting the Spirit be the Guide, be the Creator of all that comes to the aspirant. The practice of meditation and more importantly of contemplation is primary. It is following the Voice that comes to one during these sessions of contemplation that brings one to the humble position of losing the ego in the Self and living for and from the spirit. It is living the Soul's experience, and not living the body, the mind, the family, the social experience, that becomes primary. This may necessitate giving up some of the physical comforts and pleasures based on money and intellect as the means of support. All is based on the experiencing of the Spirit and following Its lead. Thus, the Mystic finally lets go of the accruements of physical living and arrives at the "Interior Castle" as defined by Teresa of Avila. It is there that Oneness, Wholeness, is experienced and the peace that passes intellectual understanding comes forth. Jesus said, "My peace I leave with you; not as the world gives it unto you" (John 14:27 paraphrased), which means a Peace that is centered in Spirit, not in intellect. It is not thought control any longer but Spirit, feeling, the affective side of their nature that guides and directs the Mystic. It, intuition, is primary and balanced with the intellect.

The mystical is such a numinous experience that it is very difficult to define. Only through Being can one fully understand the mystical Way.

The commitment of the individual is to "Go Higher" in the mystical Way. It is my belief that although many may achieve all that they long for by following metaphysical principles, they may still want to continue on the evolutionary Path so well explained by Teilhard de Chardin in *The Phenomenon of Man*. Basically the Mystic believes that *all* is based on awareness of God and the leap from thought control to letting go of all thought and following the intuitive Knowing that comes from the Spirit is a big one. But it can be taken with ecstatic results.

As to a major difference, many who follow the metaphysical Path may get off into the psychic realm. This often leads them to ego inflation as to be psychic is made so much of by others that it is difficult to be humble in the face of the adulation that the psychic gains from other people. The psychic must have other people to demonstrate to and to prove their value. Many follow this way before and after joining the metaphysical Journey but I shall not include the psychic areas of life regression, channeling, crystal reading, reliance on Ascended Masters, etc. These I believe to be in another category of the Search. The Mystic is free of the need for guidance from others.

The Mystic can be totally alone without the adoration of other people and still be at peace for it is the adoration of God that the Mystic seeks. The success of the mystical Path does not depend on the adulation of the populace. The Mystic knows the Spirit and the people around the Mystic may not realize that. The mystical is the secret Way and success thereby is judged by the ecstasy, the peace, the joy that comes bubbling up within the Consciousness to be shared when appropriate. It is Being! It is experiencing God!

The Mystic is impelled to give service to humankind. That is a part of the Mystic Path. It is taking that Wholeness, that Oneness to the world. If one does not do this it is doubtful that one is a Mystic in the fullest sense. Now in the East the Mystic may spend life separated from the world in prayer and meditation for the good of all humankind. But in the West the Mystic must serve humankind in any creative Way that is given from the Spirit. The impetus for service must be heeded.

In the metaphysical philosophy service is not always stressed. That lack of teaching about service is changing, however. Service to others takes away the selfishness that may develop as one learns to use the metaphysical direction. It is giving what one receives that makes the Flow continuous. The River of Light that comes to us must flow on to others else it will be dammed up and become foul. Reaching out in love to individuals, groups, and the masses is a necessity for the health of the individual. This could be the greatest difference between the metaphysical and mystical teaching.

The teaching of the metaphysical philosophy is easier to understand than is the mystical. As you go through this book the mystical will become more clear. Be assured that I am not suggesting that one should give up the metaphysical Way for the mystical Way until one is ready. I am suggesting that after we become adept at living the metaphysical teaching we might consider going to the mystical and combining the two.

Now we will turn to the basic philosophy of the metaphysical Way. It may not be all inclusive, but the major points shall be covered.

PART I

Chapter 2

METAPHYSICAL TEACHING

In the last chapter I mentioned that metaphysical or New Thought may be used interchangeably as relating to this philosophy. Of course, the deeper we go into it, the less "New" it appears to be, for many of the following points will be recognized as very old, based on ancient religious teachings. But in terms of the Christian movement many of the ideas will be "new." and the use of "thought" indicates a basic tenet of the movement. Controlling of the thought process, using thoughts centered on Spirit to heal, recognizing one's Divinity, and using thought in the sense of inspiration; all of these are included. The thought is impregnated with Spirit, however, or it would not be effective. And healing does occur when thought and Spirit are One.

In some circles this is called a science. Now science when defined means a system of thought, a system of going from one truth to another to reach a conclusion. It is believed by many that science implies truth but of course we know that scientific truth is always evolving. So is the New Thought philosophy. This book illustrates how it can evolve. It is believed by adherents that the Truths taught are verifiable through experience and can be replicated, both requirements of intellectual science. The metaphysical is mental science.

The following teachings of the metaphysical philosophy are very broad and will differ somewhat between groups and individuals who teach and practice them. However, general themes emerge. So let us begin, even though these items may not be all inclusive nor listed in any particular order.

- Individual thought controls what comes to a person's experience as well as into the world's experience.
- All is God. God is in every person, place, rock, plant, animal, or thing. All is Good.
- The Christ Within each person is the Holy Spirit and is God or a part of God and one's Authority.
- The Kingdom of Heaven is within each person, surrounds the earth, is right here and now. Our recognition is needed.
- The reason for the earth experience is to come into Consciousness of our Innate Divinity. That power, wisdom, love, etc. is made conscious and is the point of the Search.
- Since each person is responsible for the experience that comes to them through thought, word, or deed, projection of blame is discouraged.
- The world is not Reality. Reality is the Kingdom of Heaven.
- There is no power of evil. All is Good. So-called evil is the misuse of Good. Coupled with this is "There is no devil."
- Usually ethical or moral laws are not laid down by the New Thought teaching. The Law of Cause and Effect is stated in common vernacular as: "Do unto others as you would have others do unto you." "Do not be deceived; God is not mocked, for whatever a man sows, that he will also reap" (Gal. 6:7 RSV).
- Each one through right thinking, positive thinking, Inner Guidance through prayer and/or meditation is capable of making correct choices on social issues for one's self.
- Denials of the negative and affirmations of the positive change thought patterns in the conscious and unconscious mind.
- Metaphysical, or in other words symbolic, interpretation of the scriptures is an accepted understanding of the Bible. Historical and literal interpretation is not eliminated. The Old Testament teaching may be referred to as well as Paul's teachings, but the four gospels, the teaching of Jesus Christ, are more often stressed. Emphasis on Bible Study varies from church to church.
- The vicarious atonement by Jesus Christ as taught by traditional Christianity for humanity's sins has been understood differently. Jesus demonstrated to humankind that the physical body and death can be overcome. His teaching of "the Father within" is a foundation.

10

- Jesus Christ is not worshipped as the only Son of God. We are all Heirs of God.
- Jesus Christ is considered both human and Divine.
- The physical body is honored as the Temple of God.
- Reincarnation and Karma are accepted by some proponents or adherents to the metaphysical philosophy.
- Suffering is not necessary in order to reach the Kingdom of Heaven although suffering may serve to teach one the lesson that they need in order to go Higher.
- God is seen as masculine/feminine or Father/Mother or androgynous. Women are equally important in the Kingdom of Heaven as well as in the Church or Center. Many are ministers.
- Healing of body and mind through prayer and Divine treatment is accepted. Turning to a medical doctor when needed is also entirely acceptable as the Spirit moves through the doctor as well as the chemicals to effect healing. The healing is done on all levels—mind, emotions, body, and Spirit—simultaneously. Love is the real healing factor.
- The greatest Law for the metaphysician is the one Jesus reminded us of, "Love the Lord your God with all your heart and with all your soul and with all your mind. Love your neighbor as yourself. All the Law and the Prophets hang on these two commandments" (Matthew 22:37, 39, 40).

These are only some of the major teachings, offered as an indication or guide, although Principles accepted or taught by individual groups or organizations evolve in their own way. A deeper study of the various texts would be necessary to make the discrimination. I refer you to the basic texts listed in Part I, Chapter 1.

PART I

✳

Chapter 3

RESULTS OF METAPHYSICAL BELIEFS AND PRACTICES

So why should anyone choose to follow the New Thought Way? What are the results of this devotion to a Way of Spiritual development?

There are many who practice this teaching outside the Movement. It is certainly a minority as far as active membership in metaphysical Churches or Centers. However, more and more people are joining the Movement in one way or another. Many are not members of a Church and do not want to be. Many are affected by the books and literature that come out of this philosophy. Unity publications reach the lives of 3,000,000 all over the world.

Many books on the best seller list have teachings that include the metaphysical philosophy. *The Power of Myth* by Joseph Campbell with Bill Moyers has many metaphysical statements and is being read by many. It was on the Best Seller List of the *New York Times* for over a year. Also, the Alcoholics Anonymous organization uses prayers that are familiar to those in the metaphysical Centers. When support groups have as a central teaching, "You are responsible for your own life," and when members turn their lives and their decisions over to the care of God, this is a metaphysical (as well as a mystical) act of surrender.

Change is happening and the metaphysical movement is helping the world become more spiritual as each one experiences God within as the Christ. And as each realizes their own

Consciousness of the Divine through positive thoughts, prayer, meditation and living from the Good that they are, the change will come faster. We are really learning what it is to forgive and love with an unconditional love. That is most important.

Now let us see some of the specific results of New Thought practices. These are not in any particular order except as they have come. The importance of each depends on the Consciousness level of the Seeker.

Freedom

It seems to me that one of the greatest blessings you will experience in the metaphysical teaching is freedom, freedom to be who you are. The basic tenet, that you have a Spirit Within which will guide you in all things (John 14:26), gives you that freedom from outer rules, outer religious teachings, outer authority that you may have been taught was necessary for your salvation. If indeed your Inner Guide directs you to that outer authority, well and good, but you have the choice. You are Free to express that real Self you were always supposed to express. No church, social or outside authority will control your choices. But remember, you will have to accept responsibility for what your actions, thoughts, and words bring to you. In the long run, that is real Freedom.

Consciousness of God

It is rising in Consciousness of our true Divinity that the spiritual movement of metaphysics is all about. It is Spirit centered, it is Christ centered, it is God centered. It is organized to help the individual expand his conscious awareness of who one really is—a Divine Being who should have all the Good that God represents. It is that Truth that is at the heart of the metaphysical philosophy. And it is yours for the asking, the devotion, and the practicing of that Guidance you have from the Christ—your Inner Counselor. Positive thinking helps bring one to that Center experience.

Emmet Fox, a great teacher of the metaphysical Way, says,

> It is an absolutely vital part of Jesus' teaching that you are constantly to seek direct inspirational contact with God, constantly to keep yourself an open channel for the pouring out of the

Holy Spirit into manifestation through you. (Sermon on the Mount, page 74)

Jesus Christ

It is difficult to convey in a few words the metaphysical understanding of who and what Jesus Christ is and stands for.

Jesus Christ, according to some of the teaching, was man (Jesus) and God (the Christ) as One, and he demonstrated and taught how each of us can do the same—become One with the Father.

To some, the vicarious atonement, a traditional Christian teaching, is seen as Jesus' teaching that sin, sickness and death can be overcome in Oneness. His life, crucifixion and resurrection brought this Truth to humankind. The resurrection is seen as the purpose of the crucifixion by many teachers. The resurrection demonstrated the Spirit's victory over death of the physical life. This is true for each of us.

The teachings of Jesus Christ, as found in the four gospels, are basic to much metaphysical philosophy. The teachings of Paul are less often quoted although Paul's teaching on the Christ within is basic in both metaphysical and mystical philosophy. From Paul we read:

> To them, God has chosen to make known among the Gentiles, the glorious riches of this mystery, which is Christ in you, the hope of Glory. (Col. 1:27)

The Christ is the Consciousness of each human being. The Christ is the title given to the Inner Spirit that *is* each of us and to which we turn for Guidance for our Journey. Scripture supports this, based on Jesus' words in his prayer,

> I in them and you in me. May they be brought to complete unity to let the world know that you sent me and have loved them even as you have loved me. (John 17:23)

Emphasis on Jesus Christ varies widely in the various divisions of the metaphysically designated teachings.

Jesus Christ is seen by many as the greatest Teacher for the religious life but is not worshipped as God. Emma Curtis Hopkins, the Teacher of teachers in the metaphysical and mystical philosophy, taught Jesus Christ as basic to her spiritual guidance and understanding.

15

To follow the Jesus Christ Way will bring one to Wholeness. Each has their own Journey.

Prayer and Meditation

Prayer, that time of speaking to the Presence, of asking for boons from God, that time of quiet peace and thanksgiving, of worship, is a part of all religions and appears in many forms. It is based on faith, on desire, on thanksgiving, on communion, on one's approach to God. It usually needs words or chanted sound to express. There is affirmative prayer which is emphasized by most teachers, which contains affirmations that touch the inner Spirit of the listener. Prayer has brought forth great spiritual gains.

Meditation is not speaking so much as listening. There are guided meditations, spoken mantras, chants, singing which brings the Pilgrim to a place of Silence, silencing of the thoughts. If you are in the metaphysical movement and have not yet meditated, you will. Indeed you must. To contact that Inner Spirit and to heed the Guidance needs commitment, organization of time and duties, a quiet place away from the noise of the world, and a devotion to the One Self within.

You will find the results of meditation manifold. It is the Path to loss of stress, worry, a feeling of inadequacy. It is the only Way to go if one is seeking Guidance from the Comforter, the Christ, the Counselor, the Holy Spirit. It brings one to those goals of compassion, service, love and joy. Later in the section on Mysticism we will discuss the need by some searchers to meditate on the chakra centers in order to change the body to Light. But for now, know that you will be drawn into meditation, and you will have Peace beyond all understanding.

Positive Thinking

When your thoughts are turned from the negative affairs of the world to the positive, your Consciousness is at peace with God which is All Good.

Positive thoughts somehow bring to us the positive results we all seek for our happiness. Some have accused New Thoughters of being Pollyana-ish and perhaps it could be seen thusly. However, to be positive does not mean we ignore the facts around us. We see the facts, and know facts are not Spiritual Truth. We do our prayer work, we commit to involvement in improving those conditions, and then "let God." We do not need to struggle or work hard for the improvement of our or another's lot in life. It is through letting go of concern, anger, resentment that we raise the condition to a higher vibration and the result may be the opposite. This sounds crazy, I know. But it has been proven time after time.

Resist not evil was the teaching of Jesus, and we have seen Gandhi put this into practice. When we respond to a negative we give it power—nonresistance makes it crumble.

So positive thoughts bring positive results. It is a cardinal rule of this teaching.

A book that would help you understand this was written many years ago and by the testimony of the author, Norman Vincent Peale, was based on the metaphysical teaching of Positive Thinking. It is titled *The Power of Positive Thinking*. As a testimony to his book, learn of the life of Norman Vincent Peale. He is still going strong at more than 91 years of age.

Imagining and Visualizing

Another result of your metaphysical experience will be the ability to imagine some good coming to you and then expecting it to come forth. We all imagine, we all visualize what we want to experience. If we are worry inclined, that of which we are afraid usually happens. Imagining the Good that is coming to you is a priority for successful living. What you think, you envision. To spend time in visioning the positive coming into your life is effective. Earnest Holmes, Founder of Religious Science, teaches,

> There comes to each the logical and exact result of his own receptivity. To each, life brings the reward of his own visioning; to the one all is pure, to the righteous all is righteous; and to the good all is good. (The Science of Mine, p. 442)

Results from visualization are more often achieved when it goes beyond pure intellect and a deep emotional feeling accompanies it. A true Vision seen by the physical eyes usually comes upon one unexpectedly and is often born from a deep emotional need. Imaging is usually not apparent to the physical eyes although the results may be.

Acting on what we visualize is also needed for in acting as

though it has come to pass, we give energy to that which we desire and the Universe responds.

If the need to imagine, to envision, is attractive to you, so be it. You should envision only the good, true and beautiful. Be careful what you envision!

Denials and Affirmations

Denials and affirmations are very helpful to one who is on the metaphysical Path. Our mind, usually, is jam packed with negative, worrisome, sad, guilt-ridden thoughts when we start our interest in a new spirituality. These negative thoughts can be denied and positive thoughts practiced by an act of Will. You will learn early that you are in charge of your life and your thoughts. Positive thinking, as previously stated, is a hall-mark of the entire movement.

To get rid of the negative set of the mind one can repeat, over and over, a denial of the seeming reality of that particular belief or habit. This is an intellectual exercise which must be accompanied by deep feelings to be effective.

Then an affirmation of the Truth as seen from a loving, peaceful attitude is repeated over and over. The process is one where thinking will gradually turn to positive and thus our mind is reprogrammed.

Coupled with this is a continuous monitoring of one's thoughts, words and actions. *Belief* that these exercises will be effective is basic to success. In time you will be surprised at how much more positive you have become. And a better, happier, freer life will prove it. (See *Lessons in Truth* by Cady.)

You will learn that denial may be misused if you deny the fact that a negative experience has happened to you or exists in your life. Some people are prone to cover up the admission that something, some relationship, some socially-induced activity is not good for their spiritual advancement and must be changed. Denial will not work if it is a cover up for some refuse in your life that needs to be admitted then done away with or not accepted as needed for your Consciousness growth. Facts need to be admitted. Facts may not be Spiritual Truth but may be blocking your Way to Spiritual Truth. One thus denies the power of these facts to control one's life.

There are those teachers of this Way who do not believe

18

that denial is necessary but that affirmation is. In fact they teach that to deny gives strength to that which is denied. To affirm the Good, they say, will allow the subconscious to become full of the recognition of Good and no negative can enter. It is affirmation of Spiritual Truth that is important. One teacher states that in the very act of affirming, one is denying a belief, a condition, a seeming fact. So in affirming, one really denies power to the opposite.

Cause and Effect

The Law of Cause and Effect is considered a basic Law in most metaphysical teachings. What you sow, you will reap, to put it simply. Innate in this Law is taking responsibility for the experiences that come to you. To accept this takes a very deep breath and a great leap of faith. Faith in the Guidance of God to help you learn from the Law of Cause and Effect will gradually allow you to make the right choices. And Grace often comes in and helps you out of the experience. It is taught that the Love of God is Omnipresent and ready to bring us through whatever experience we choose. The Law of Cause and Effect, if you believe in it, will help shape your human choices to spiritual choices.

A caution, I feel, should be added about application of the Law of Cause and Effect to what happens to others. No love is expressed when one sees a seeming tragedy happen to others and then dismisses it with, "Well, they brought it on themselves." The Law must be mixed with compassion and forgiveness if it is to lead higher.

Many adherents to this Law can carry a tremendous load of guilt if a negative event happens in their life. The metaphysical teaching points out that the Law lovingly applied is a positive guide for our Journey. A feeling of guilt can often push us to look at ourselves, our behavior and encourage us to "clean up" something we are doing. And then the guilt needs to be let go of. Understanding and compassion for one's self and others makes this Law more workable. Grace is always present.

Karma and Reincarnation

Another important awakening for you may be the idea of reincarnation and karma as Spiritual Truth. All metaphysical philosophies do not teach these Eastern and now Western religious ideas. But if you accept that the Goal of the worship of God is to recognize your Oneness with Divinity, you can more readily embrace the concept that this is not the only life you have in which to "make it." It seems such an impossible task for many to earn the right, after this life, to enter Heaven at death given the propensities of human behavior. But to realize that the gains you make in this life will carry over into the next incarnation is an encouraging belief, to say the least. It removes lots of guilt and fear of dying. This teaching in Western metaphysics excludes transmigration of the soul into an animal—only into a human body does reincarnation apply.

Karma has been usually understood as the "evil we do lives after us." Karma, however, when defined, takes on a more positive perspective. That talent which you develop, the good you do, the strides you have made toward perfection are also carried into the next life. Enlightenment is an evolutionary process.

Yes, you may have some suffering, you may have some relationships to clean up that have resulted from past life actions, but all of that will teach you and will elevate you to a higher level of awareness if you see it in that light. Eventually, the Grace of God will wipe out all the negatives and you will not suffer for past mistakes.

Prosperity

How about prosperity? Will I have abundance if I choose the metaphysical Way? Will my physical needs for money be taken care of? Will I need to work? Can I just live on the flow of the Universe bringing to me all I need financially to support me? We live in a materialistic society, where do I fit in?

All of these questions and more are asked by the neophyte. Sometimes the questions are more important than questions about physical health. Sometimes the most pressing need is for money.

What can you expect by way of prosperity? What is taught about it? What do you have to do to bring it? Do you have to be limited in physical comforts to live the metaphysical teaching?

There are many ways to express prosperity or abundance. For some, abundance is expressed as love from God and people. For some, abundance is expressed through a happy experience of Life itself. For some, it is just Knowing the Christ that is abundant living. But for some, it is a beautiful house, a pink Cadillac, a trip around the world, or to be known as a wealthy person. It all lies in the personal desire, Karma, and one's soul's Journey.

To express abundance or prosperity will require one first to really believe that Spiritual Substance is the basis of all in the Universe. When one accepts this, that God is Omnipotent (all powerful), Omniscient (all knowing), Omnipresent (all present), then with this spiritual mind one may have all they need or desire. In those desires one may make mistakes, though. However, if abundance is really sought then to follow Jesus Christ's words will bring it to them.

These are,

> Therefore I tell you do not be anxious about your life, what you shall eat or what you shall drink, nor about your body, what you shall put on. Is not life more than food and the body more than clothing? . . . But if God so clothes the grass of the field, which today is alive and tomorrow is thrown into the oven, will he not much more clothe you, O men of little faith? Therefore, do not be anxious. . . . But seek first the kingdom of God and his righteousness, and all these things shall be yours as well. (Matthew 6:25, 30, 31, 33 RSV)

There is the answer. *There* is where prosperity comes from. Seek the Kingdom of God, think the Kingdom of God, and you shall receive. This is the metaphysical as well as mystical Way.

Tithing

Tithing (giving one tenth of one's income to the source of one's spiritual good) is taught by some but not insisted upon or made a rule or an edict of the Teaching. Freedom of choice in giving is a tenet. Love offerings are very popular for classes and seminars. Many teach as Jesus taught, to give liberally. Although Jesus did not mention tithing as a law, he did say that every thing that one gives will be returned to the giver, and more.

Give, and it will be given to you. A good measure, pressed down, shaken together and running over, will be poured into your lap. For with the measure you use, it will be measured to you. (Luke 6:38)

Tithing is an Old Testament teaching. "Test me in this," says the Lord Almighty, "and see if I will not throw open the flood-gates of heaven and pour out so much blessing that you will not have room enough for it" (Malachi 3:10). This refers to tithing.

Many seminars and classes have set charges. Giving on a Love Offering basis means you will give as your heart directs. This is very popular and takes a dedicated student to give with open heart from one's abundance. There are Commitment Celebrations to support some churches. Others depend on the usual offering taken at the church service. "As you give so shall you receive" is a reminder often spoken. One's spiritual commitment is involved in the level of one's giving either of money, time, or talents to the source of one's spiritual good. Giving often rewards the giver more than the receiver.

Relationships

Your relationships will get better and better, more fulfilling, and with more peace! How is that for a promise? Well, of course, this depends on you and how deeply you go into Being with your Inner Spirit. At first the Guidance may be confused, or you are confused in receiving it. Relationships fulfill one of our most vital needs—Love. And sometimes it is hard for us to choose those that will bring us their promise, or to whom we can give our love.

You may find you need changed relationships. You may have to give up some if you are really serious about your direction in the metaphysical Way. Inner Guidance will bring the right relationships. Changes may occur which on the surface are painful but in the long run will bring you much more happiness.

Later you will find that fewer relationships are needed and that those you have will most often be with those who are like-minded.

Health and Healing

Two branches of the metaphysical teaching were founded by those who had a spiritual healing of a physical ailment that doctors could not heal. These were Unity, founded by Myrtle and Charles Fillmore, and Divine Science, founded by Nona Brooks and Malinda Cramer. You will find that spiritual healing is one of the main tenets of all metaphysical teaching. Counselors, practitioners, spiritual healers are trained and are available from most Centers. Some who are adherents to the metaphysical Way may find their talent lies in healing and do not need the formal teaching offered.

Spiritual healing is undertaken on request. The one being healed may have some realization of the Spirit for it to be successful but this may be unconscious. Some very wonderful healings have occurred from the prayer work of spiritual healers. There are written testimonies that verify them.

Health, based on the needs of the body, is not a main thrust in the teachings, but is assumed by the interest in healing of individuals. However, the health that one develops is based on one's own choices. As one raises Consciousness of the Spirit the vibrations of the body change and different foods, drink and exercise may be required. The body is the best guide to what your health requires if you are Centered. You will learn to listen to it.

Support groups for those who are involved in addictions to drugs, alcohol, and others are organized by many of the Centers. Counselling for emotional problems is also available although the serious cases are usually referred to a professional counselor or psychiatrist.

Available also are national and international 24-hour prayer centers with a staff of spiritual healers who pray around the clock. Freewill offerings are gratefully received.

Guilt

One great Good that comes from the metaphysical philosophy is letting go of guilt over past sins (mistakes).

When we accept the Law of Cause and Effect, having realized that we have brought to ourselves the feelings of guilt, more and more of the mistakes will be eliminated from our lives. Also, our conscience, which is often based on ego, will be transformed into Consciousness of God, the Talisman. We will find that the metaphysical philosophy does not lay down rules for us as an individual. The teaching is to help us make the choices for ourselves that will bring happiness and Good to our lives. But we make the choice. Holding the feeling of guilt over the head of the miscreant is not something we will hear in classes or sermons. We make the decision as to what is right for us. Morality will become our responsibility and the right choices will be made for us and for others in our lives. Having been reared in a Christian society, most of us will have a set of rules for right conduct that are pretty similar. Freedom of choice and understanding consequences have kept more people on their Path than accusation of wrong choice ever has.

Know that all is Good, and no matter what your mistake, some Good can come from it. Ask for forgiveness from Self as well as others, discipline yourself to not repeat the error, and go on your way a free unburdened soul.

Forgiveness

What about forgiveness? Is it any different in this world of metaphysics than it is in the traditional Christian world? Probably not except in those traditional beliefs that God forgives us through the institution of the Church, and that is a pretty big difference. God loves us, does not hold anything against us. God is love. We do not need to ask for love and forgiveness except to cleanse our own conscience. If we feel we have separated our personality from our Christ, our Self, through some act or some word or thought, then a prayer of forgiveness may be in order and is addressed to our Inner Spirit. The God of the Universe is impersonal but our Inner Christ is very personal. We are really forgiving our self, our ego, our personality.

Divine harmony and perfect Love is taught. The Lord's Prayer is important, and it says "Forgive us our debts as we have forgiven our debtors." So it would appear that we must first forgive and then Spirit forgives. In giving forgiveness, we receive forgiveness. When understanding is gained that all is Good then we can see ourselves as well as others as having just made a mistake. Peace, harmony, and healing can then take place. Healing often requires a forgiving attitude.

Forgiveness is a type of denial. It is clearing of the negativity so the positive can bring forth our blessings. Love is the basis for forgiving, and to practice Love is our reason for Being.

So "clearing the decks" of guilt by forgiveness is taught. And you are the prime mover to do this. Self responsibility is continuously affirmed, and Love is your Guide.

And, of course, asking another to forgive you for some harm you may have done them is important in order to be in harmony with all others. Admitting to God, to your Self, and to another the wrong you might have imposed will clear the Shadow that is over your Soul so that Light can shine through.

Love

And what about Love? Will one become more loving to one's self and others? Will you be any more loving than the vast majority of those dwelling on this planet? Well, it depends on you.

Metaphysical teaching can be misunderstood as a selfish way to prosperity, health, and good relationships for the individual. Love that accompanies these good results is a must. Without love, all the denials and affirmations, all the positive thinking, all the loss of guilt and fear would be nothing. It is dependence on Love of God that motivates and supports us. And as we become more Centered, Divine Love will take over the thoughts, words, and actions of the individual and Love will be the foundation of our life. We define God, among other definitions, as Love, and the end point is to become fully conscious of our Oneness with God. And so we are striving toward, we are relaxing in, we have trust and faith in Love. For Love is our Goal and our Way.

Devil, Evil, Hell

Among teachings of which you will lose your fear are the concepts of the devil, evil, and hell. If you embrace the metaphysical philosophy and put it into action in your life, these three teachings found in many religions will hold no more fear for you. That is a shocking statement for many. Metaphysical teachings do not accept a power of evil, a being called the devil, and a place where sinners will go after death to burn forever and forever.

The *devil* is a reflection of humanity's anthropomorphic view of God. Humankind has seen God as a reflection of itself. We have placed on God our own projection. And since we are in a state of duality we see the devil and evil as a bal-

25

ance to the Good. This is a hold over from the Old Testament teaching of two powers, Good and evil, God and devil, Heaven and hell.

We have within us our ego, often our Shadow, that needs transforming by the Spirit. but our choices and our behavior are within our control and it is not "The devil made me do it." That is a weak statement. To recognize our strength we should affirm "I am a loving child of God, and my choices bring my Good to me." The devil is an excuse for our mistakes. Belief in evil as a power accompanies the idea of a devil. There is only Good! There is only God!

Evil, it is taught, is the absence of Good. Evil is not a power unto itself. Evil is the misuse of the Good that we all are. The Spirit is misused. Our own choices bring seeming "evil" into our life. The shadow within our unconscious needs to be confronted, to be cleaned out, to be acknowledged, but it is not a power that Good cannot transform.

Hell is not even mentioned in some of the metaphysical texts. It is suggested by some that it is scriptural error in translation. Hell is sometimes thought of as a figure of speech and refers to the suffering an individual may have over some error. Hell is not taken seriously and therefore you will not look to a time after death when it may await you. A loving God could not condemn anyone to such suffering forever.

Let us remember that God is Love, Joy, Peace and our awareness of God will give us that. We may choose to have something less, but we can escape from it by prayer, meditation, change of thoughts and faith in God. Earth living can teach us to find Heaven.

Heaven

And speaking of Heaven, what will we learn about the Kingdom of Heaven?

Jesus made many references to the Kingdom of Heaven. And he repeatedly said that it was within us. The Kingdom of Heaven (God), he said, is not here or there, but the Kingdom of Heaven is within you (Luke 17:21).

We are to experience Heaven here in earth life. That may take a little time, lots of Centering on the Inner Self, a change of attitude from the outer guidance to the Inner Guide. But the

Kingdom of Heaven is all around us. "Look up and see." It is a statement of mind, it is a state of Grace. It is yours. You do not have to die to go there.

Bible Interpretation

The emphasis on Bible reference in sermons and in classes varies with the metaphysical teachings. Some emphasize it more than others. If you do not find reference to scripture, Jesus Christ, and God comfortable because of past conditioning, you can find a Center that soft pedals this teaching. In some teachings the Bible is basic, and both literal and metaphysical interpretations may be used.

If metaphysical interpretation of the Scriptures, which means symbolic interpretation, rather than literal interpretation, attracts you, then you will find much benefit from books that interpret the Bible thusly and/or from classes and sermons presented at these Centers. (See Bibliography for such books, especially Elder.)

Christian

Now you may be asking at this point, Is the metaphysical philosophy Christian? A good question, for New Thought philosophy does not follow traditional Christian teaching that Jesus died on the cross for our sins and thus we receive salvation, a basic Christian tenet.

New Thought philosophy has removed all the fear and condemnation for sins that were and are used to "shape people up" in traditional Christianity. Also New Thought interpretation of scripture is different. Interpretation is based many times, not on an historical or literal basis, but from a metaphysical symbolic understanding. Scripture has deeper Truth than appears on the surface.

Jesus is a Wayshower and a Savior but not the Savior in the Christian sense. It is his teaching understood from a deeper level and an emphasis on some of his teaching that the Christian church has not followed, that is different.

New Thought philosophy has in it teachings from many other World Religions. The commonalities in these religions form many of the basic tenets of its teaching. But basically it is entrenched in a "New" interpretation of Jesus' teaching.

The Inner Guide of the Christ and the teachings of Jesus make it Christian, I believe.

Omnipresence

This is the teaching that God is in everything. This may be hard to accept, especially when we have been smothered by the belief that God is "out there," not "in here." Now, the knowledge that each person has a direct connection to God has been around a long, long time. At least 2,000 years when Jesus said, "Ask and it will be given to you; seek and you will find; knock and the door will be opened to you" (Matthew 7:7) and "And I will ask the Father, and he will give you another Counselor to be with you forever—the Spirit of Truth" (John 14:16,17a). How plain that is!

The Christ, the Holy Spirit, is always present. Your life will be filled with prosperity, friends, love, health and joy as you turn within in meditation and follow the intuition that awaits you. And that is also the beginning of the Mystic Path.

The three "Omnis"—Omnipresence (everywhere present), Omnipotence (all powerful), and Omniscience (all knowing)—are stressed. Much study of them will raise Consciousness.

Women

The New Thought philosophy does not discriminate against women being leaders in the Church or Center. The world is open to women and men in the metaphysical organization. Women are accepted without prejudice into each of the ministerial training schools. The large percent of licensed practitioners of healing, counseling, teaching are women.

The movement away from the patriarchal society and patriarchal God is coming faster and faster. Much of the choice of accepting God as the Universal Substance, as being nongeneric, is up to the particular minister. The phrase Mother/Father God is popular although "Our Father which art in Heaven," the beginning of the Lord's Prayer, is sung in most church services.

The movement toward allowing the feminine in both men and women to express and to be a teacher of spiritual Truth is strong and expanding rapidly.

Many husband and wife teams are ministers in Centers or Churches. The balance of the masculine and feminine in the church organization is a real plus for the congregants.

Death

The teaching on death in the New Thought movement, like some traditional Christian teaching, is that the physical dies but the Soul lives. And since we are Spirit, in reality there is no death. Memorial services in metaphysical Centers stress the life that is still Being. Those who wish to accept reincarnation know that the Soul will choose another body and continue on the Journey to Oneness in another lifetime.

The term death is often changed to "transition" or "the soul has gone on to the next experience."

Your Bliss

When one practices meditation, learns to listen to the intuitive guidance from the Spirit Within, one will be directed to that occupation, to that task, that will give such Joy that the idea that it is work will flee. Sometimes, if one is new to meditation, the intuitive does not come immediately. But after you remove the blocks to the idea of change and to knowing your life purpose, then the nudging will become almost a command. And when it happens, you will know it is Truth for you. Of course, if you follow your Bliss, as Joseph Campbell puts it, it may mean major changes in your life, your job, your associates. But when you are led, when it is perfectly clear what you are to do, it will be easier to make the changes. Finding out what you came to this life to accomplish will add a new dimension to your life.

Our basic task, of course, is to move through our experiences to Oneness with the Divine Energy we call God. That is our Bliss. But many in metaphysical teachings are not ready to take that Mystical step. In the meantime, they can find their Bliss in their work, their service, and their relationships with others.

Most of what I have covered in "Beliefs and Practices" has dealt with you as an individual. You may be wondering if this teaching is basically for the individual and not for the society in which one is living. Well, it is true that it starts with the individual, but it ends in the Universe and all that it encompasses. To start with the individual seems to be what is needed. This is a practical teaching and can be applied to the world of the individual. As the individual comes closer to the infinite Being that interpenetrates all, then the effect will be spread out into all the world. Raising of the individual consciousness will affect everyone around us and beyond.

Taking this consciousness into the world may make one more compassionate, more involved in movements for Peace and more aware of the needs of the entire Planet. Many are in the environmental movement, the peace movement, and other humanitarian causes. For those who are less inclined to action based on their belief, there is the teaching that the raising of Consciousness through meditation will automatically affect others and the entire world. It is taught and believed that we are all One Mind. We are Omnipresent, as the Universal Spirit.

We have, insofar as possible in a short discourse, covered the teachings and the beliefs as put forth by the New Thought Movement. There is more, and if you are interested there are a multitude of books, tapes, and videos available as well as classes to attend at Centers and Churches. Worship services are held each Sunday. Since this is an individual Path, each of you will find your own answers, your own Way.

So now, let us turn to a discussion of the Mystic Way. If you have been practicing the metaphysical Way you have a fine foundation, for it leads easily into the Mystical Way. However, there are some who are not destined to tread that Way in this lifetime. To really accept and follow the metaphysical Way can be a lifetime challenge. It might even include several lifetimes.

When we find ourself in the Mystical Way we are usually ready for it. Or it might slip up on us as it did with me. Sometimes we are unconsciously ready for it and do not know it. There are greater plans made for us in the Spirit than we can ever imagine in our human consciousness. A major purpose of this book is to help those who are ready to take the next step into the Mystical Way.

Jesus Christ and the Mystics who have gone before us have given us the guidance as well as the example. We can handle it for the Christ always accompanies our Journey. The narrow way leads to Life. The broad way can lead to destruction. Choose Life! Jesus said, "Whoever finds his life will lose it, and whoever loses his life for my sake will find it" (Matthew 10:39). Jesus was speaking of the Christ (my sake). When we Center in the Christ for our choices, we find Life, and that is the Mystical Way!

Are you feeling unfulfilled? If so, let us explore the Mystical Path together and see if that is your Way.

PART II

✳

Chapter 1

MYSTICISM

Mysticism is a way of life. It is a pattern of behavior, of action beyond the ordinary way of living on planet earth. It, the mystical Way, is undertaken by a small percent of people, but the number is growing as the metaphysical movement becomes more popular and a way of life for many. The numbers will also grow as the Christ Spirit within each is recognized and comes to full flowering. It leads to the End Point. It is the reason for the Soul's Being. It is God. It is Universal Love. It is all there is. It IS. And if you have been practicing the metaphysical philosophy, you may be ready for it or are already in it and have not given it recognition.

I am aware that these are very abstract terms for many. The terms lack meaning. It takes something besides intellect, the thought process, to understand. It is an experience of the spirit and cannot be of the intellect alone. To understand depends on intuitive realization. It is right brain activity.

Many are fearful of the term and what it implies. They see the Mystic Path as one of giving up all pleasures of the senses, living in poverty, being a recluse, having no interest in world happenings and people. It may appear to be a selfish Path for one's own happiness. A giving up of some of their family and friends is foreseen. It appears to be a lonely and sacrificial Journey.

Each Mystic is free to choose the Path that is right for their soul. This may include following a Guru's direction. Eventually, however, to be a true Mystic one will have guidance only from the Inner Knowing. This Path is dictated by the Inner Soul, the Soul that is calling each to Oneness with God, that Universal Energy and Love that we have named God. Each Soul is unique, not like any other. Thus each Path will be unique. And following that Path is living an authentic life.

Some who choose the Mystic Path may be guided to live as the first part of the former paragraph describes. But some in our modern New Age will be guided to experience an ordinary physical life with comfortable surroundings, with beauty of art, music, nature, and very adequate means to take care of physical needs. They may live in the midst of the city and be aware of the needs of society although not bowed down in anguish over the pain the majority of humankind is going through. They will be *in* the world but not *of* the world. They will observe God at work in all worldly happenings.

The rise of interest in the mystical Way is inevitable, I believe, because the Mystic Way is based on intuition, wisdom, creativity, love, feelings. And all of those are classified as feminine. To bring forth the feminine in our largely masculine dominated world requires not only the finer use of the intellect but allowing the Spirit to break through from that Inner Awareness which we may have so long neglected. Interest in the feminine is also being born in our awareness of the needs of Mother Earth. The balance is showing forth.

The Mystic becomes more and more androgynous as intuition is allowed to come forth to balance the intellect, which is masculine. Indeed, the feminine, being creative, often feeds the intellect the thoughts which bring into existence that which intuition has inspired. When a person becomes androgynous (balanced both in the feminine and masculine), their physical needs change, their emotional needs are balanced, and creativity shows forth. This, androgyny, is a part of and the result of the Mystic Path.

To be a Mystic is really a very natural human/spiritual Way of expressing. It should not be reserved for very few. It is really being that authentic person that one is meant to be. It is co-creative with God. It is living your vocation. It is being the Heir of God.

My definition of mysticism does not include the occult, spiritualism, hypnotism, or magic. A Mystic does not have to rely on these activities to understand one's self and others. One's Path is laid down by the Inner Knowing from the Spirit. There are those who do not understand this because of lack of experience. They may define mysticism as a pathological condition. The true Mystic is the sanest of human beings.

F. C. Happold, in his book *Mysticism, A Study and An Anthology* (page 42), says, "The urge to know through mystical intuition is not the same urge as that which is the impulse in the search for scientific and metaphysical knowledge. The kind of knowledge that comes through *intuitus mysticus*, unlike scientific and metaphysical knowledge, has a 'saving' quality; it leads to 'eternal life'."

"This is eternal life," said Jesus, "to know God and Jesus Christ, whom He has sent" (John 17:3, paraphrased).

Our view of the Mystic has often been colored by the accounts of the Catholic Mystic who lived in a monastery under monastic orders, doing servile labor, assuming poverty and chastity vows and chanting the Catholic canon all day. Some (very few) of these monks and nuns became mystics. Our definition of a Mystic must change as we go into the 21st Century when more and more will join the metaphysical movement or will come from the traditional Christian Churches and eventually become Mystics.

The Mystic, in my simple definition, is one who commits their life and all they have to the Guidance of the Christ within and carries out that Guidance in acts of service to humankind. For the modern Western Mystic it is not a matter of going to the woods, or to a cave and meditating on the Good in order to lift the Consciousness of the world. This is not a requirement but may be chosen by some for it is a great service and is a giving up of the physical pleasures of the senses. If the Guidance is thus, then one should follow. But forcing oneself to live an austere, ascetic life because some saint or Mystic has done so is not always following the Inner Guidance.

Sometimes, usually for many people, the Mystic life just opens up to one, gradually, step by step. It takes a certain introversion of personality to affect this—introversion based on meditation and solitude. However, there are extroverts who balance their personalities by withdrawing from much interaction with others and choosing to be alone more. Introversion and extroversion become balanced in the personality, as do all opposites, the further one goes on the Path.

The Mystic:

- yearns for closer and closer Unity with the Reality, with God
- hungers and thirsts for righteousness (right-use-ness)
- finds the deep hunger fulfilled by more and more contact with the Divine through meditation and contemplation
- lets go of the ego, the small self, as the guiding force in their life
- transforms many egotistic interests in the practical matters of the world to Spirit Realization
- finds Divine Love is the leading component of the Search and the Goal
- serves all of humankind while being directed by Spirit
- may have a Light and/or Voice experience which is most Real and cannot be explained by logic or reason (from R. M. Bucke's *Cosmic Consciousness*)
- finds the mystical Experience inexpressible in words; how-ever, often uses writing, art, music, invention, or poetry to express

Once a person has tasted the Light and Love of Ultimate Reality, they are hooked, they are devoted to the Mystic Path. They may discount it for years, their life may contain many ups and downs, the old way of living may be clung to, but eventually they will return to that moment of High Ecstasy of experiencing the Christ Light and/or Voice through medita-tion, prayer, or just during a moment of disconnecting from the rational mind. They will remember that moment as the most meaningful Real moment of their life. Sometimes they can avoid response to it all their life, but in the next life or the next, it will return.

The world needs Mystics. There are many people who would not claim that they are Mystics. They feel this is too high and holy a name to be known by. But if they have had that Mystical Moment of complete Oneness, they will never be the same, and if they are meditating deeply, they have had or will have that Moment.

Meditation and contemplation are a must if you are inter-ested in reaching these high mystical moments. However, meditation comes in many forms, and a person who does not even know the meaning of the word may in a period of deep silence experience that Divine Moment.

To continue on the Path, it will be necessary to practice a form of meditation, for it is through stopping our rational, logical thoughts that we may reach that Silence, that ineffable Silence from which all knowledge comes. The Mystic knows, "All is God," and the Intuitive Knowing of Truth is a part of the Glory that the Mystic Path brings.

Many are inadvertently becoming Mystics through meditation. There are so many in the West who are new to meditation now and have no idea where it is leading them. The same may be said of those who practice yoga and various spiritual exercises that are faithfully undertaken. Little by little they are balancing into Oneness the body, the emotions, the intellect, and the Spirit. They may reach a high measure of ecstasy that Pure Love brings and not know where to go with it. When they allow the Guidance to come through, they will choose the Mystic Path eventually.

The need, mostly unconscious, for this high experience is becoming so strong in human beings all over the planet that many are resorting to artificial means of drugs and alcohol to experience it. Once having had the "high" they are hooked and must have more and more of the substance to achieve the "high." This "high" is not long lasting and often brings disaster to the participant. But it is the Spirit seeking them and their need to seek the Spirit that is being played out, I believe. Use of drugs is *not* the Mystic Way.

Many recognize the Source of Ecstasy, drop the drug "high," and start their search for a Spiritual High. The Spirit will break through one way or another, and it is becoming more insistent during the turn of the Century. Many find that Spirit through the Alcoholics Anonymous Teaching and support groups based on the Twelve Steps of the Alcoholics Anonymous program. However, the need for group involvement to maintain the spiritual Journey may eventually be transcended for the individual Path of Mysticism. The Mystic cannot be too dependent on others. The Spirit within, around, and through the individual must become the Guide and Support of each life.

In the accounts of the Mystics, both autobiographical and

biographical, they often speak of the glory of a Light vision usually coupled with a Voice of the Inner level. This experience gives them a direction, words of love, sustaining strength for overcoming. In our Bible we have accounts of such: Moses, Abraham, Adam and Eve, Jacob, Isaiah, Ezekial, Jeremiah, Elijah, Elisha, John the Apostle, Peter the Apostle, Paul, John the Revelator, are some of them. The Bible is for everyone whose background is Jewish or Christian, no matter what their level of understanding or seeking. Much of it is for the Mystic's guidance. When we read of a Bible character, such as Job, who had learned to live his life centered on physical accomplishments, loses everything, and then has a Vision and a Voice experience, we have a mystical experience described.

There are many books that give accounts of Western and Eastern Mystics through the ages. These books include:

Mysticism, by Evelyn Underhill
Cosmic Consciousness, by Richard Maurice Bucke
Ordinary People as Monks and Mystics, by Marsha Sinetar
Silent Fire, by Walter Holden Capps and Wendy M. Wright
Mysticism, A Study and Anthology, by F.C. Happold
What Is Enlightenment?, by John White (Editor)

Accounts of these lives may give us clues as to how our Path can possibly unfold. However, each Path is directed by the Inner Self. A particular "map" for our Path may not be the experience of another. A Mystic living in our modern world may have very different experiences and overcomings than the Mystics of 500 years ago, but basically the Journey is the same—the complete realization of our Divinity. For the beginning is *that* Oneness and the end *is* that Oneness. We only need to recognize it.

The aspiring Mystic may have to make some hard choices pertaining to their earth life. But these changes usually come gradually. The Spirit is always there to guide and support.

When one meditates for years it may change the cells of the body to more Light through the actions of the Kundalini energy (see glossary for definition). Thus the body becomes En-Light. This offshoot of meditation is not realized by many. The changes of the physical, help the Mystic let go of habits that might interrupt expansion of Consciousness. The feeling nature also changes. There is an emptying of the conscious and unconscious mind of the negative accumulation. All is cleansed and the material body is changed to the spiritual body. (See Paul's message in I Corinthians 15.)

Eastern religious Mystics usually practice some form of Yoga. Yoga is for the express purpose of bringing together the body, the mind, the spirit into a state of Oneness. Along with this is the raising of the Kundalini energy through the various channels of the etheric body to open different levels of Consciousness as well as to change the cells of the body. This energy either finds rest in or opens different chakras which are whirls of energy said to be located near the endocrine glands of the physical body. As this energy courses up the spinal column it touches these centers. The teaching is that eventually the Shakti Energy becomes One with the Shiva, Universal Energy, and enlightens the body as well as brings into Oneness the Soul and Universal Energy. The last is in Western terms.

Breath control, various physical exercises, meditation on Divine Consciousness, commitment to the All, contemplation on a deep level are all practiced to bring about the change of the physical body to a higher form, to pure light. In the example of Jesus, as well as Eastern yogis, we have a demonstration of the physical becoming pure Light. Consciously undertaking the raising of this Serpent Fire, the Kundalini, is usually done under the guidance of a teacher, a Master, or a guru. No negative results can then accrue. (See *Kundalini, The Evolutionary Energy in Man*, by Gopi Krishna.)

Giving up certain associates; changing of work; undertaking service filled projects; letting go of love of materialism as the main focus of choices; studying scripture and books; living, eating, dressing simply; and being creative in some endeavor—all of these and more may be your Path.

But it is not giving up, it is gaining All. For the Mystic who is at One with God has All.

"Letting go and letting God" is sometimes the most difficult step for the Mystic at the beginning level. The person who has been in metaphysics for years may not have taken that leap. Before the leap they may have become a meditator, or may have had a spiritual experience of the birth of the Christ. Then faith in God's Goodness gives them the will to continue the Path no matter what. They KNOW that only Good can come to them. Sometimes this leap of faith is tentative, and when the aspirant pulls back through fear they may have some deep challenges. But when they finally let go of personality control, of ego control, and lean back with Faith on the Grace of God, they will know God. For to KNOW God is to let go. It is a beginning and an end.

Fear of change motivates many who are tentative about following the Path. This feeling will be demolished when Faith takes over. Following the Inner Christ can bring only Good, no matter what the change may be.

And the Mystic is steeped in love, but a love that surpasses personal love, personal feelings for friends and relatives. This Love takes in the whole world, indeed the entire Universe. It does not discriminate as to race and color. It does not dictate what is best for another. It does not control. It frees everyone and everything to be who and what they are. The motto is "Let Be."

Just because one has chosen to be a Mystic does not mean they are a Mystic. "To be" is a verb. When one reaches "I AM a Mystic" the life of that person will be different. The Mystic on the path learns to BE. It is To Be the life from the Center at all times which raises the vibration of the mind and body and one ultimately reaches Ascension. Jesus is our example.

Jesus Christ—how do Mystics of the Christian persuasion deal with Jesus Christ? It is known that before his Advent there have been other Mystics in other religions. It is accepted that mysticism has been a way of life for some Shamans, some Hindus, some Buddhists, some Muslims, some Jews, and others. Jesus Christ did demonstrate beyond them in his Resurrection and Ascension. But there have been other crucified "gods" before him. And so how is he different?

Religion throughout human history has been evolutionary. Great Truths have been enunciated by great beings, and the advancement of humankind on the road to Perfection has taken place. At the time of Jesus' birth the then known world needed a teaching that circumvented, went beyond, the Law that had been laid down by the Jews. The masses were following blindly their edicts. There seemed to be no individual spiritual connection with God for the majority. And so Jesus came representing the Father, the name he gave to that great Power we still do not fully understand. He came and taught beyond the Law of the Jews, for the Law was stagnating the evolution of Consciousness of the adherents. Eventually the expansion of the Consciousness of humankind resulted. He came to a small region, according to the Bible account, but according to the *Aquarian Gospel of Jesus Christ*, he traveled throughout the world and taught and had Initiation. Thus he touched all the religious leaders of the then known world. His teaching was a great advance over previous human religious beliefs. My understanding of His teaching, however, is based on conventional Scripture.

We who are from a background of Christianity accept Jesus as our pattern to find our mystical Journey. He exemplified God and human as One. He had true knowledge and understanding; he KNEW love of and union with God; and he practiced the mysticism of action, of taking his KNOWING to the populace. He said, "It is the Father in me who is doing the work" (John 14:10). He knew Who he was. He was the Mystic Incarnate with the Word. He did not turn from tough decisions and go into his cave. No, he openly addressed the ills of the world. He did not deny them as being a part of the human experience. He turned them into opportunities for advancement on the Path. He was human and Divine, at One.

Our day is not the same as 2000 years ago. However, the Mystic can find a place of service to lift humankind to a higher awareness of the Spirit. Any service will be based on the inherent desire of the Mystic to remove blocks from the Path to Oneness for each individual and ultimately for all. This, the Christian Mystic sees, is the Way of Jesus Christ.

It is a gigantic assignment. But remember, it does not have to be done in a day. We have Eternity.

My Path came upon me without conscious choice. So much of the Mystic Path is mysterious. Our phenomenal mind is unable to grasp what is happening. And more importantly it, the mind, cannot always express what has happened for many of the experiences cannot be described in words. This is a common declaration by the Mystic. It does not make the experience less true, however, for to the Mystic it is the most *true* experience that can happen to a human. It is inexplicable. One has to experience it to Know It. And Being It for maybe only a few seconds, minutes, or hours is the Morning Star to guide the Mystic, forever.

We are each divided between wanting to be individualistic and being One with the All. The experience of Intuitive Knowing, Oneness with All that is, is what each human longs for.

It is said that each human being is a Mystic. By that is meant that each of us consciously or unconsciously is searching for the Ultimate Reality which brings happiness, joy, Ecstasy of Pure Knowing. Over the centuries we have attempted to find that Summit through many human theories of God and the relationship between the individual and God. Jesus brought us an example of the Ultimate Dream of All. And we are restless until we find our Self in God.

This expansion of Consciousness of All That Is cannot stop now. It will continue on, our step-by-step realization of God will continue on, until we all reach that Omega Point of Teilhard de Chardin (see *The Phenomenon of Man* by Teilhard de Chardin). And so the Mystic Way is leading us to that point. However, it may not be the final evolutionary Journey that humankind needs. But it is the highest and best we know of now.

PART II

Chapter 2

MYSTICS THROUGH THE AGES

There are many books written *about* Mystics. There are books that have come down to us through the ages written *by* Mystics. The whole subject of mysticism and Mystics is coming to light. We, the people, are now privy to the idea of mysticism. Its time has come for us of the 20th Century and the 21st Century.

I shall discuss and quote from some of these Mystics that have gained recognition through the ages. Some Seekers have not been so recognized. Many were not recognized as Mystics until hundreds of years after their death. Catholic Mystics had to be recognized by the Church in order to be authentic. Some were granted Sainthood by the Church.

Because mysticism has been such a mystery it has been misunderstood, and many Mystics were considered insane or at least mildly odd. Few modern people want to acknowledge that they are Mystics, and those who are Mystics have often not been recognized.

To define who or what a Mystic is presents a problem. During their lifetime they may not be recognized, and since they are very humble, they would not claim that place. Later their writings, their life, their influence on others may bring them recognition. My simple definition of a Mystic for choices made in this chapter is one who has had an illuminative Light and Voice experience and/or served humankind and God.

The Protestant movement has not encouraged mysticism, but now, with the broad movement toward Inner Spiritual devotion and guidance that has resulted from meditation, this is changing.

In the Eastern religions we have writings from Mystics and about the mystical Path. The Upanishads, the Tao te Ching, the Bhagavad Gita, the Buddhist Suttras all have writings that point toward the path and the Goal. Tibetan Buddhism has taught for thousands of years about the existence of the place of Shangri-La or Shambhala where Perfection reigns and which will eventually spread over the face of the earth. The Koran has teachings of the mystical Way. The Old Testament and the New Testament have books that are deeply mystical and direct the Seeker on the Path. We Christians can learn from our own Scriptural teaching, and from the Mystics, then we follow our own individual Path.

There are many wonderful examples of a true Mystic. From these I can choose only a few. These have spoken to my understanding and needs. At the end of the chapter I shall list some of those books written by or about Mystics from which I have read and learned.

My choices could come from Eastern and Western Mystics. However, the Christian Mystic seems to be my favorite and therefore my choices are weighted in that direction. Some Mystics cannot be classified as either Eastern or Western for they are a blend of both.

Because I believe that Jesus Christ is the greatest Mystic, I shall devote an entire chapter to his teaching on the Beatitudes. The teachings gleaned from those will be in terms of the understanding of the Aspirant who is on the Path.

The Buddha

The Buddha was no doubt one of the greatest Mystics. He lived about 500 years before the advent of Jesus. His teaching was first given in India and has spread worldwide. His leaving wealth, family, and possessions to follow the Majestic Path when he was Prince Gautama Sakyamuni led him to join some ascetics as a monk. However, that did not fulfill his need for Knowing. After other heroic experiences, he found reliance on his own Inner Light, the Four Truths, and the Eightfold Path which have been taught to millions throughout the world. This has led them to a deeper understanding of their Buddha nature within. This and more gives him a place as the Buddha in my Hall of Mystics.

After the Buddha wandered around trying to find the answers to life's riddles, he determined to sit under a fig tree (called the Bo-tree) and meditate until the answer came. It is said he fasted and was subject to many temptations from the spirit world which he overcame. He had a deep desire for Enlightenment. When he knew that his deep desire for Enlightenment had prevented him from receiving it, he gave up all desire and the Light shone. (Bodhi means Enlightenment.) According to some authorities he had a struggle about whether to keep his Enlightenment to himself and live out his life and eventually go into Nirvana at his death, or to go back into the world and teach what he had learned. We know the choice he made. This giving up desire for Enlightenment is important for us, too. It will happen when it happens. Don't lead. Follow.

Buddhism has been divided into so many branches and sects as a result of different interpretations of his teaching that the basic teaching may have been watered down. (This sounds like what happened to Jesus' teaching, doesn't it?) Joseph Campbell believed that the teaching of the Buddha and of Jesus Christ was very similar when cleared of the interpretation by organized religious groups. (See *The Power of Myth* by Joseph Campbell.)

The Buddha taught that the Eightfold Path would lead to the state of no-desire or Nirvana (Enlightenment). They are: (1)Right Belief; (2) Right aspiration or purpose (overcoming sensuality); (3) Right speech; (4) Right conduct (love all creatures with a right sort of love in word and deed); (5) Right means of livelihood (obtaining one's livelihood from work consistent with Buddhist principles); (6) Right effort (discriminating between wise and unwise choices); (7) Right mindfulness (well disciplined thought habits); (8) Right meditation. (From *Man's Religions* by John B. Noss, p. 134.)

The metaphysical philosophy has been influenced by the Buddhist teaching along with the teachings of Jesus Christ. You will recognize these eight steps as being very mystical. He, the Buddha, has affected your world, and mine also.

Moses

Because Moses was the founder of the Jewish religion and because Moses had the subjective Light and Voice experience, I classify him as a Mystic. He made a mark on the world that changed the history of the entire human race.

Moses "saw" the burning bush in the desert and "heard" the Voice of God giving him Guidance to save his people. He followed that Inner Voice with one exception (Numbers 20). He freed his people from bondage, and he gave them the Ten Commandments, a covenant between God and the people. These Ten Commandments, if followed, would get them into the land of Milk and Honey (Heaven, Shambhala, Nirvana).

It is noted in Exodus 34 that after Moses spoke to God, and He spoke to him, Moses recorded on stone tablets the Laws that God gave him. When he came down from the experience, his face was so radiant that the people were afraid of him. He showed his En-Light.

He was a Mystic, and he served humanity at the direction of the Lord's command.

The metaphysical philosophy has, likewise, been influenced by his teaching as recorded in the first five books of the Old Testament, the Pentateuch.

Jesus Christ

(See Part II, Chapter 3)

Paul

Paul, the great harbinger of the Christian Church, was no doubt a great Mystic who was willing to live the Truth of Jesus Christ and die for it. He had a great Light and Voice experience as he journeyed to persecute the early Christians (Acts 9:3-9). He was struck blind and eventually was healed through spiritual healing. He carried the message of Jesus Christ, of the Christ within, far and wide, and died a martyr, so far as we know.

I have chosen to quote his description of the effect of the state of Enlightenment on each person. All of I Corinthians 15 relates to resurrection from the dead, not only the spirit, but the physical body will be resurrected. Verses 50-55 follow:

46

I declare to you brothers, that flesh and blood cannot inherit the kingdom of God, nor does the perishable inherit the imperishable. Listen, I tell you the mystery: We will not all sleep, but we will all be changed—in a flash, in the twinkling of an eye, at the last trumpet. For the trumpet will sound, the dead will be raised imperishable, and we will be changed. For the perishable must clothe itself with the imperishable, and the mortal with immortality. When the perishable has been clothed with the imperishable, and the mortal with immortality, then the saying that is written will come true. "Death has been swallowed up in victory. Where, O death is your victory? Where O death, is your sting.

This I interpret symbolically, not literally, to mean that at some time our body of flesh and blood will change to pure Light and Death will be overcome forever for the one so changed. This is the stage of Being One when our mystical Path has taken us to this Glorious Goal which is often described in other Biblical passages.

Paul's Christ was that Inner Voice that directed him and he followed. His teachings have served millions upon millions of humanity for 2000 years. And although often misunderstood, the foundation of the Christian philosophy seems to rest on his teachings. His task was to advance the Cause of Jesus Christ and to enlighten *all* men and women.

John the Apostle

John had his own Light and Voice experience in the presence of Jesus the Christ. He was present on the mountain of Transfiguration with Peter and James. They had been taken there by Jesus. They saw the three, Moses, Elijah, and Jesus, changed to Pure Light, and then they heard the Voice, "This is my Son whom I love, with him I am well pleased. Listen to him" (Matthew 17:1-5). After this John was ready to do a great work although he did not understand what he had seen or heard. This is most often true of us also.

The Gospel of John, the Books of John 1,2,3, and the Book of Revelations are thought, by some, to have been written by the Apostle John, although there is some division on this. The Gospel of John teaches the mystical Path, especially John 14-17. Jesus, in those passages, gives guidance to the apostles to turn to the Comforter within, that which we call the Christ.

In the Book of Revelations we have an account of John seeing the Light Vision and hearing the Voice (Revelation 1). He then proceeds to teach the Mystic Path to those who can understand the Book symbolically. This Book has been misinterpreted many, many times as being frightening and predicting dire results if one does not follow the Way as interpreted by some Christian theology. My book, *Revelation for a New Age*, interprets it symbolically. John directs us to the Path of the Mystic and also describes the human way of mistakes of life and finally shows us triumphant at the Throne of God where Enlightenment is described.

John walked the Path. In 1 John 4:7-21, we have his great discourse on love. Love is the Path. With all our intellectual strivings we cannot reach that Mystic Marriage without Love. Love is the Beginning, the Path, the Goal. He said, "God is love." "Whoever does not love does not know God, because God is love" (1 John 4:8). For love is what all Mystics demonstrate. Love and Service—that is the Mystic Way.

Teresa of Avila (1515-1582)

This wonderful woman Mystic is perhaps my favorite Catholic Mystic. She speaks as a woman. She wrote to women, the nuns in her Convent.

She lived in the 16th Century and was a Spanish Carmelite nun. The outstanding book that she wrote, among others, is *The Interior Castle* in which she describes the Mystic Path. It is a classic in mystical literature. The Castle is described as being of seven layers or seven circles with the Journey being from the outer to the Center where the King, the Christ, abides. (See Part III, Chapter 1 for description of these seven stages.)

She describes the conflicts in our life that keep us from making progress to the Interior of the Castle. She makes suggestions for overcoming the "serpents" that are in our unconscious which might detain us. She mentions the Darkness that may come over us on the Journey, and she always carries along the Love and compassion of her Lord. She speaks of the extreme challenges that may confront us in the sixth house or level and then describes the Glory of the seventh level or the Center. The ecstasy of the Spiritual Marriage is beautifully described. Her main point, "And the Lord accompanies us all the Way," is reiterated often.

In 1555, while in chapel, she had her enlightening experience of being addressed by interior Voices, of seeing Visions and experiencing Revelations. She had struggled for years with the conflict of "the world and of God." This experience resolved the conflict and she was totally devoted to Jesus. Her service goes on and on as those in and out of the Catholic church find her teachings very inspiring and helpful on their mystical Path. Her book on prayer, *The Way of Perfection*, is easy reading and gives excellent directions for the meditator.

Swedenborg (1688-1772)

It is said that Emmanuel Swedenborg influenced Ralph Waldo Emerson, Thomas Troward, Carl Jung, Ernest Holmes (one of his mentors was Troward, who studied Swedenborg), William Blake, Elizabeth Browning, Bronson Alcott (father of Louisa May Alcott), William Butler Yeats, and many others. I wonder why he is not spoken of in metaphysical circles, this man who lived in the late 17th and early 18th Century. He was a genius in the minds of many.

Swedenborg was from a Lutheran family, his father being of the clergy. He was scientist, engineer, a clairvoyant. He taught that all in the creation is Divine. The Inner Soul is the Guide for each of us. His interpretation of scripture was based on symbolism. He wrote many volumes on science and on metaphysics and was one of the first to explore the unconscious through dream work.

His Enlightenment came at the age of 54 as he was exploring the location of the Soul in the human body. His writings came from Inner Knowing. It is said that he owned no books when he was doing his religious writing.

Swedenborg never married, was highly educated, lived a simple life after his conversion, and was a vegetarian. He inspired many and certainly served humanity through his voluminous writings and their influence on the metaphysical, psychological, and Bible interpretation scenes.

Emma Curtis Hopkins (1853-1925)

Emma is called the Teacher of teachers, and she influenced so many by her classes and her writing that we owe her a great debt of gratitude. Five who were founders of major metaphysical churches—Ernest Holmes, Charles and Myrtle Fillmore, Nona Brooks, and Malinda Cramer—were taught by her directly or indirectly. Her last and greatest work, *High Mysticism*, puts her into the hall of Mystics. It is written to and for those who are or aspire to being a Mystic.

Biographical material about Emma Hopkins is sparse. She never spoke of or wrote about her personal life. Neither did she reveal anything about personal mystical experiences. Her writings reveal those, however. She was born September 2, 1853 and died in 1925 (the date is unverifiable). In 1883 at age 30 she joined Mary Baker Eddy, founder of Christian Science. Hopkins was editor of the Christian Science magazine but separated from Eddy's organization in 1885 because, it is said, Hopkins believed that Truth comes through many religions while Eddy believed it came only through her.

She wrote a metaphysical, symbolic interpretation of the Bible. She also wrote a book on healing titled *Scientific Christian Mental Practice* and many other books which have been published since her death. Her greatest book is *High Mysticism.*

I have chosen Hopkins as a recognizable Mystic because of that book. It is written from the authoritative center of her God Consciousness. She writes from that High Level of Knowing which she exemplified in her teaching to the founders of Unity, Religious Science, and Divine Science.

Her teachings are vast but are centered around the Christ Within each person and throughout the Universe. She taught that when one's thoughts are directed toward the All, there is no more sickness, sin, or death. The Universal Solvent, as she calls God, penetrates all. All is Good. God is Good, there is no evil. "Look up," she often states, "There is only Truth."

As I have said, we do not know about Hopkins' mystical experience, but we do know that outcome of her service to humanity. Millions have been affected by her teaching. She is the ultimate New Thought Mystic.

Mrs. Hopkins founded a ministerial school and a healing ministry in Chicago. She healed many, directly or indirectly, through her students. The metaphysical movement was definitely given over to healing ministry in the early days of its founding. But Emma would not want it or us to stop there. It is being One with All that she emphasized as a Mystic and told us how to achieve it.

Evelyn Underhill (1875-1941)

In his book, *What Is Enlightenment?*, John White includes Evelyn Underhill as one of the Mystics. She was English. Her most well-known book is *Mysticism: A Study of the Nature and Development of Man's Spiritual Consciousness.* In this book she devotes much space to women Mystics as well as men. She calls the mystical life the Unitive Life and says there are five stages on the Path (taken from *What Is Enlightenment?*, John White, p. 44):

(1) Awakening or conversion
(2) Self knowledge or purgation
(3) Illumination
(4) The Dark Night of the Soul
(5) Union or Unitive Life

Underhill uses as illustrations of these five steps the writings and life histories of many Mystics. The Unitive Life, she says, although lived in the world, is never of it. It is on another plane of existence. She was like Emma Hopkins in this as we see Emma bringing this point forward many times. Evelyn points out repeatedly that the Mystics cannot describe the Unitive Life in words. It is ineffable, the experience of Ecstasy and Joy. And this Spiritual Marriage of the Soul with God can only be experienced, not explained.

Evelyn Underhill includes much psychology in her explanation of mysticism. She quotes from the writings of many Mystics and explains how psychology and mysticism can be combined (shades of Carl Jung). The Mystic, she says, is Being, not knowing or believing. Being is fulfillment of love which is the Mystic's own Place.

Carl Jung (1875-1961)

Although Carl Jung is not always classified as a Mystic, insofar as I am concerned he meets the qualifications, simple though they are, that I have set forth.

In his autobiography, *Memories, Dreams, Reflections*, Jung describes several personal Light and Voice experiences. His service to modern day humankind is just beginning to take hold as Freudian psychology fades away.

His first conversion experience occurred at about 12 years of age. He then came to the realization of a new birth, of the

Truth that "now I am myself." Previously, he says, "Everything had happened *to* me. Now I happened to myself . . . now I exist, now I will." (*Memories, Dreams, Reflections*, Carl Jung, p. 33.)

> Once I emerged from the mist (the mist preceding the illumination experience) and became conscious of myself, the unity, the greatness, and the super human majesty of God began to haunt my imagination. (Memories, Dreams, Reflections, p. 32)

During an illness and near death experience visions of the Mystic Marriage and the Dark Night of the Soul were experienced during the recovery period. High Ecstasy and Joy accompanied the experience; a vision of the consummation of the Mystic Marriage between Zeus and Hera came to him; and the room was impregnated with what Jung called "sanctity." All of these are definite indications of a Mystic's experience of Wholeness. At the death of his wife he had the experience of detachment from relatives and emotional ties (p. 289 ff).

Jung called his Inner Voice Philemon, one who represented superior insight. He learned to listen to his inner "guru" who gave him many illuminating ideas.

And, of course, his service to humanity has just begun as more and more spiritually minded people recognize Dr. Jung as a teacher of the metaphysical as well as the mystical Way. He has thousands of followers who combine his teaching on the balance of the masculine and feminine and the recognition of the Archetypes in dreams as factors in healing. He talks of the Transformation of the ego to a higher knowing and the end point of Individuation which is the mystical Goal. His statement of purpose is to help people realize that the Spirit is the central point around which a Good life can be built.

Jung was born July 26, 1875, and died June 6, 1961. His father was a Protestant clergyman, and Jung observed that he early on was given guidance about the inadequacy of the religion of the church. But his deep Knowing of God shows clearly through the transparency of his work.

Matthew Fox (1940-   )

Matthew Fox, a truly contemporary Mystic, came to my awareness through his book *The Coming of the Cosmic Christ*, published in 1988. I see him as a Mystic for his teaching on mysticism definitely places him in the category of Mystic. He Knows from experience.

Fox is a Dominican Priest, and after the publication of this book he had the "Vow of Silence" imposed upon him by the Catholic Church for the year of 1989. I know nothing of his own mystical experience, but am sure his deep-seated devotion to the Mystic and mysticism is evidence of his own mystical experience. He speaks of the historical Jesus as the Mystic and a teacher of mysticism.

Fox says about his book, "It is about the awakening to mysticism that alone, I believe, offers us hope for the healing and a deep spiritual conversion" (prologue, p. 2). He writes that a shift from the historical Jesus to the Cosmic Christ is necessary. Scripture is quoted to support his Truth. He also addresses the problems of the ravishing of Mother Earth as connected with the Patriarchal religion in which we have been caught up. The rising of the feminine in Consciousness is balancing the masculine perspective that has so long dominated us. He maintains, "The coming together of the historical Jesus and the Cosmic Christ will make Christianity whole at last" (p.7).

He sees Jesus as the teacher of mysticism, and calls mysticism the "Resurrection Story of our Time" (p. 35).

Matthew Fox's book will become a classic, I believe. He has written several others which will also move seekers along the Mystic path. His emphasis on the teachings of the Mystics, Hildegard of Bingen and Meister Eckhart, shows forth in his works. He is a Mystic of our time. He has much to teach us if we are interested in the Cosmic Christ which is moving through everyone on this planet.

No account of the lives of the Mystics can ever be complete. Each researcher, each author, can only choose the few who speak directly to them. Thus I have done. There are many, many more who have much to teach us. But I believe the ones chosen here give us a fair example of those who have gone before us, or who are contemporary with us, to show us the Way.

Please know that you are not alone if you have chosen to pursue the Mystic path. The Spiritual guidance of Mystics of the past is here and now. Their thoughts are our thoughts, are One. God is seeking us as we are seeking Him. And the Christ within us personified in the life and works of Jesus moves in our hearts and in the hearts of humankind. If you have chosen the Path, you are in the forefront of a great movement toward the Realization of who we each really are, God incarnate. Each of us, Mystic or metaphysician, is being called.

These are just a few of the books available to teach one about the various Mystics of the Ages. These are some I have referred to in this writing as well as some I have not referred to. Some are reviewing the Mystic Path. Some are accounts of the Mystics who have lived the Way. (See Bibliography for publishers.)

Bucke, Richard	*Cosmic Consciousness*
Capps and Wright	*Silent Fire*
Elder, Dorothy	*The Song of Songs and Enlightenment*
Fillmore, Charles	*The Twelve Powers of Man*
Fox, Matthew	*The Coming of the Cosmic Christ*
Hopkins, Emma Curtis	*High Mysticism*
Ramakrishna Vedanta Center	*Women Saints, East and West*
Sinetar, Marsha	*Ordinary People as Monks and Mystics*
Underhill, Evelyn	*Mysticism*
Van Dusen, Wilson	*The Presence of Other Worlds* (Swedenborg)
White, John (Editor)	*What Is Enlightenment?*
Happold, E.C.	*Mysticism, A Study and An Anthology*
Jung, Carl	*Memories, Dreams, Reflections*

PART II

Chapter 3

THE MYSTICAL TEACHINGS OF JESUS THE CHRIST ON THE BEATITUDES

We need a pattern to follow although the Comforter, although our Christ, the Holy Spirit, is our Primary Teacher. But being human, and Divine, it helps us to know what others have experienced on the path. Since the Christ is the same in us as well as in Jesus, our Primary Teacher is the greatest Mystic, Jesus Christ. So we shall discuss some of his teachings before going to the Beatitudes.

> I am the Way, the Truth and the Life. No one comes to the Father except through me. (John 14:6)

This is the Christ speaking. In Christian New Thought terms no one comes to the Father except through the recognition of, centeredness in, and following of the Guidance of the Christ Within. Jesus exemplified that way.

> If you love me you will obey what I command and I will ask the Father and he will give you another counselor to be with you forever—the Spirit of Truth. The world cannot accept him, because it neither sees him nor knows him. But you know him for he lives with and will be in you. . . . On that day you will realize that I am in my Father, and you are in me, and I am in you. (John 14:15–17, 20)

This, of course, is telling us that the Christ, the Spirit of Truth, is in us and as we follow It we will see the Father. Seeing the Father is becoming One with the Father, Jesus' name for that Energy we call God.

The account of Jesus' transfiguration into pure Light is recorded in Matthew 17. He had taken three of his disciples to a high mountain where he was transfigured and the Light and Voice experience came to them.

> There he was transfigured before them. His face shown like the sun, and his clothes became as white as the light.

And in Matthew 17:5:

> While he (Peter) was still speaking a bright cloud enveloped them (Jesus, Moses, Elijah, Peter, James and John) and a voice from the cloud said, "This is my Son, whom I love; with him I am well pleased. Listen to him." (Parentheses mine)

The three disciples who were with Jesus on a high mountain had a Cosmic Consciousness experience in this Light and Voice experience. In most accounts of Mystics, they too have the Light and Voice experience. Some of those were Moses, Elijah, Elisha, Jesus, Paul. Many have these experiences but, just as the disciples, do not understand them. These experiences may be a part of our Journey. These experiences can be an opening to the Mystic Path.

After his resurrection, it is written, Jesus appeared and disappeared instantaneously. He could take on the physical body again as he demonstrated when he asked for a piece of fish and ate it (Luke 24:40-43). He was able to go from one level to the other. He took on a Light body and ascended which means he went to the highest Spiritual level, but he is also with us. This Ascension is the end Goal of the Mystic as we understand it.

The Mystic believes the scripture:

> I tell you the truth, anyone who has faith in me (the Christ) will do what I have been doing. He will do even greater things than these, because I am going to the Father. (John 14:12) (Parentheses mine)

This scripture is a directive to us on the Path which indicates that we, too, can resurrect and Ascend. We all resurrect in Consciousness when we awake from the seeming dead and come alive in Christ Consciousness. Our Ascent is on the Mystic Path.

Two more quotes from Jesus Christ which indicate his Wholeness:

> I am in the Father and the Father is in me. (John 14:11)

> I and the Father are One. (John 10:30)

That is our Goal as mystic—*Oneness with the Father.*

THE BEATITUDES
Matthew 5:1-10

BE-ATTITUDES: These statements speak directly to our attitude and have always been most important in the Christian teaching.

The Sermon on the Mount was not spoken primarily to the crowds, it would seem, for we have "Now when he saw the crowds he went up to the mountainside and sat down. His disciples came to him and he began to teach *them* saying," (Verses 1,2)

We find this Sermon in Luke 6:20-49 also. In Luke 6:17 it is indicated that a multitude of people may have been present. But Verse 20 says: "And he lifted up his eyes on his disciples" and gave the Sermon.

The Beatitudes were the prelude to the Sermon on the Mount, and it would appear from this scripture that he taught the Sermon primarily to his disciples. Going up on a mountain symbolizes a high state of Consciousness. And "he sat down" would indicate that he was in a meditative state of Consciousness, a deep contemplative space. The disciples were far above the crowd in Consciousness but not Mystics yet. In all religions the deepest truths are reserved for the initiates. The masses are taught at a different level. For as Jesus said, after the disciples asked, "Why do you speak to the people in parables?" he answered:

> The knowledge of the secrets of the kingdom of heaven has been given to you, but not to them. Whoever has will be given more, and he will have an abundance. Whoever does not have even what he has will be taken away from him. This is why I speak to them in parables: "Though seeing, they do not see, though hearing, they do not hear or understand." (Matthew 13:11-13)

So I feel we should understand these Beatitudes with the heart and not totally with the intellect, which is how they have often been discussed. It is with the one eye (the third eye which symbolizes wisdom) and the inner ear (which listens and records what intuition speaks) and the heart (which symbolizes feelings of love) that we should read and understand them.

Let us then study these Beatitudes from the Mystical view.

1. Blessed are the poor in spirit for theirs is the kingdom of Heaven. (Matthew 5:3)

The Lamsa interpretation of this Beatitude is, "Blessed are the poor in pride, for theirs is the kingdom of Heaven." (*The New Testament*, George M. Lamsa, p. 6.)

Poor in pride, of personal ego, is where we must be if we are to inherit the Kingdom.

The Mystic has transformed much of his ego, his pride in what he can do personally, into the spiritual Knowing that all comes from the Source, from God. It is the Spirit that goes all through us, and even when we believe we personally have accomplished something it is a fallacy, for the ego is God also.

Until we let go of the intellect as our master we will not be ready for the Kingdom of Heaven. It is not the intellect that is our strength, it is our intuition, our feeling nature, that supports the intellect. The Mystic Emma Curtis Hopkins says that thought follows intuition when we are at the Mystic stage. When we realize that God is All, not separate from our thoughts, we will be ready for the Kingdom of Heaven.

The person on the metaphysical level is usually still into "What you think will come to you." That is a good place to be when we are starting the metaphysical Path, but to be in the Kingdom of Heaven we must let go all pride in our intellect, in what our thinking has brought us. We must know that all is from the Spirit. When we are perfect in this Knowledge we will be in the Kingdom of Heaven, right here and now. Notice the scripture—*not will be* but "theirs *is* the Kingdom of Heaven." Then Grace covers all.

There is much scripture given to pride. "Pride goeth before the fall" is well known. Other scripture is "pride binds them as a chain," "pride brings contention," "pride goes before destruction," "pride will bring a man low," "woe to the crown of pride," "my soul shall weep for your pride," "those who walk in pride He will humble," "the pride of the heart deceives." And finally from I John 2:16: "For all that is in the world, the lust of the flesh, and the lust of the eyes, and the pride of life, is not of the Father, but is of the world." (RSV) John was a Mystic and is speaking to us, Mystics all.

Perhaps we should also discuss Spiritual Pride. The poor in spirit could mean that we must not allow ourselves to be over-confident that we have "got it made." At some level of our Journey we may believe we are further advanced than we are. The moment things seem to be going perfectly in our life we may decide, "I have readily brought all of the good to myself by my devotion to God. I am ready for Ascension." Then it is that we may have the Dark Night of the Soul. St. John of the Cross, a Mystic, has written a book on this subject. (*Dark Night of the Soul*, by St. John of the Cross.) Through the Dark Night we learn more of who we really are. We let go and trust God to bring us through.

Spiritual Pride can be a great stumbling block. We need to realize that the Path is the Infinite Way, and we may be a long way from the Mystic Marriage. At the same time our Being is activated in all that we do and we should be Self confident. Knowing, however, that there are "more mountains to climb" will cancel our Pride.

2. Blessed are those who mourn, for they will be comforted. (Matthew 5:4)

Now what would a Mystic mourn about?

Remember we are at a high spiritual level when we receive the true meaning of Jesus' teaching of the Beatitudes.

The Mystic does not mourn. The Mystic experiences losses but sees them as opportunities. Opportunities for Spiritual growth. Mourning has always been considered the human lot. But Jesus the Christ taught that we do not need to mourn over the loss of a close relationship or the loss of property when we are a Mystic, for we are detached from all relationships and possessions. There is no mourning. So what does he mean?

Emma Curtis Hopkins teaches that when one is a Mystic one need not suffer. Indeed there is no suffering, sin, or death in their life. If this is so, why should they mourn? They are above mourning for their Comforter, the Holy Spirit, is a close and immediate ally and comfort is theirs.

As mentioned previously, Mystics, most of them, speak of the Dark Night of the Soul that is a part of the Mystic's Journey. This Dark Night comes on unexpectedly and often is the darkest just before another step toward Wholeness, Oneness with Divinity occurs. Loss of contact with the Inner Divinity is one of the symptoms, as well as the inability to meditate. Seeming separation from the Source, and deep feelings of depression may come to one. But they all report that they are comforted and the Dark Night, when the Joy is veiled and the shouts of Glory are quieted, does pass.

This time, according to John of the Cross, "That which this anguished soul feels most deeply is the conviction that God has abandoned it, *of which it has no doubt*, that He has cast him away into darkness as an abominable thing." (Quoted in *Mysticism*, by Evelyn Underhill, p. 389.) Deep depression may result.

But Jesus says that you shall be comforted. And what do the Mystics do in the face of such Darkness?

They hang on. They continue to reach *out* to God. They continue to reach *in* to God. They pray even though the words seem hollow. They look at themselves and decide whether something thought, said or done could have brought this curtain of Darkness between them and the Soul's Essence. The Dark Night may bring their greatest Knowing, their deepest Being. They are comforted. And they wait on God's Grace. God is All.

And comfort comes! Jesus' promise is true. The mourning passes, and they are in the Center of God's Love, according to their accounts. They are not separated, they are one.

And finally the great book of mysticism, The Book of Revelation, indicates that when one reaches the completion of their Journey, "I saw the Holy City . . . God will wipe away every tear from their eyes. There will be no more death or mourning or crying or pain, for the old order of things has passed away." (Rev. 21). All shall be comforted indeed!

3. Blessed are the meek, for they will inherit the earth.
  (Matthew 5:5)

The meek, who are they? What personality characteristics do they exemplify? For generations the Christian was taught that meekness meant to be long suffering, submissive, servile, especially if you were a woman. But I see the meek as those who are non-resistant, gentle, seeing the Good in all, giving all authority to the Christ within. It is utter yielding to the Spirit. This is the Path of the Mystic. Meekness brings strength, not weakness.

Some interpret meek as being humble, being low and unpretentious. But I do not see the King of Glory, which we all are potentially aware of, in that way. In a spiritual sense each of us is God. Would that infer a lowly position?

Now, meek is a willingness to listen and follow the Inner Guidance. Meekness is "turning the other cheek." Meekness is knowing that a soft answer turns away wrath (Prov. 15:1). Gandhi was meek. His pacifist attitude was difficult for the military power establishment of the British to understand. But his meekness, his pacifism, turned the tide and freedom came to the Indian nation.

Meekness is a feminine trait, and men sometimes find it more difficult to practice than do women. That is why Gandhi's example has affected the lives of so many men. In meekness, they saw strength, not weakness, not submission to overwhelming power. It is yielding, not submission.

Jesus said, "I am meek and lowly in heart" (Matthew 11:29 KJV) and "My yoke is easy and my burden is light" (Matthew 11:30 KJV). And Jesus inherited the earth!

What does it mean "Inherit the earth"? Aren't we trying to get away from the earth thinking, earth consciousness?

Earth symbolizes the feminine quality of creativity, abundance, growth, sustaining strength, beauty, fulfilling physical needs. All of these are of the earth.

The earth is our home until we are ready to drop the physical body or ascend in Pure Light. We need the earth. We joy in what the earth gives us. It is not the earth that faults us. It is our own thinking about the earth Consciousness that brings us our troubles.

When you are on the Mystic Path you will eventually have all that earth provides for your physical life. Abundance, relationships, joy, peace, love. All of these are available while we live on earth. Jesus says you must be "gentle," though. Not aggressive, not competitive, not fighting for each of these blessings. But gentle, and lowly of heart.

"The earth is the Lord's and everything in it, the world, and all who live in it" (Psalms 24:1). All of the gifts of the earth are ours as we "Let go and let God." That is the result. Being gentle, noncombative, non-controlling, dependent on our intuitive Knowing and not on our intellect, this is the meek path, and we shall have all the earth provides. We will be cared for.

There is no concern about taking care of physical needs, no concern about lack of Beauty, no concern about our earth life being just right for our spiritual growth, our evolution. All the earth will be inherited by us.

It is true, our desires will change as we go our Way. Our desires for the physical comforts that earth provides will change. Our physical needs will become less and less important. Many who are devoted to the Mystic Path are guided to give up the comforts of personal home, an assured food supply, the many garments to wear and the mechanical conveyances which are so much a part of our society. All of us are not guided to take these steps, but we are guided to give up anything that distracts us from our path. And the earth is ours and the fullness thereof.

The meek, not the powerful, will inherit All.

And compassionate understanding is certainly a part of being meek. "There but for the Grace of God go I." A Love of the Christ in each, no matter what their behavior, denotes meekness. The gentleness, the kindness, and seeing the Good in all is compassion, a feeling *with* the other one.

4. Blessed are those who hunger and thirst for righteousness for they will be filled. (Matthew 5:6)

Remember we are interpreting these in terms of mystical understanding. Again, who is the Mystic? It is one who has turned all toward God, has accepted Being God, has let go and let God, and is guided by the Inner Voice daily, hourly, minute by minute.

Some questions: What is righteousness? Is it descriptive of right choice and action as laid down by the church, parents, or society? Is it the right-use of something? Is it to bring us the merit of a great reward? What is righteousness?

What does Jesus the Christ mean—hunger and thirst for righteousness? Is it an inherent drive for us to need righteousness? Will it lead us to our Goal? Let us see.

Is the Mystic on the Path to be filled with righteousness?

We have heard others called righteous with a rather critical tone of voice. We have heard of self-righteous people which when defined means those who believe they have all the answers for everyone. But Jesus did not mean that.

> But seek first his kingdom and his righteousness and all these things will be given to you as well. (Matthew 6:33)

This scripture reiterates and gives us the clue, the key, to understanding this Beatitude.

The Mystic is seeking the Kingdom. Indeed, everyone is seeking the Kingdom either consciously or unconsciously, I believe. It is seeking for Good, and God is Good.

Sometimes we get tangled up in understanding what is Good, but all believe they are choosing the Good or are choosing the way to the Good. And what is Good? For the Mystic, it is Oneness. It is right-use-ness. Right-use-ness is God inspired.

We hunger and thirst for God until we put God first in our life, and then we are filled. Then all, yes, all will be ours. Our desire to realize God fully will be filled. But note, it is *His* righteousness, God's Righteousness and that comes from our Inner Knowing.

To hunger and thirst spiritually is an ever continuing desire until we find our God Self in the Silence. We are blessed as we put God first in our life, and we are filled with right-use-ness of our God talents, of love, of joy, of right loving relationships, of all we need for physical comfort. And most importantly we are filled with the Spirit. Our every thought, word, and deed is filled with Love which is the Spirit, and then we are filled.

Jesus is saying, "Don't give up. Continue to seek, to hunger and thirst for God, and you will be filled with completion." The Mystical Marriage will be consummated. You are filled with Spirit. You are One.

As we fill our hungering and thirsting for the Kingdom and His righteousness it will necessitate many changes in our life. We give up our allegiance to thought control and turn to Spirit control. We may give up our allegiance to a particular interpretation of this Beatitude as taught by some church theology. To fill hunger and thirst will require some preparation, some planning, some choosing.

But this one pointedness will bring fulfillment. You will be filled! Jesus said so.

5. Blessed are the merciful, for they will be shown mercy. (Matthew 5:7)

Do unto others as you would have others do unto you. Oh yes!

That is the Law. It is called retribution by some. It is called "just desserts" by others. It is called the "Law of Cause and Effect." It is called the "Law of Karma" and the "Golden Rule."

This, however, is a positive statement, not fear filled. Show mercy and you will be shown mercy. Mercy is divine compassion and is a result as well as a cause of believing in One life. This will take a bit of explaining.

The Mystic sees All is God. Emma Curtis Hopkins teaches this over and over. It takes a high level of Consciousness to accept this. If we see in the beggar or the murderer anything but God then we are denying the Holy Spirit in that person. All is God. All is One. The Mystic comes to this realization as TO BE becomes the primary motive for one's life. TO BE is to see the world and all in it from the viewpoint of One who is above the world and throughout the world.

Mercy, what is mercy? Real mercy is based on love, on compassion. Mercy is compassionate treatment of one who has offended us or anyone else. It is forgiveness. And what an important aspect of our spiritual growth. Forgiveness. Forgiveness.

For-giveness is for-giving. It is for giving to another (and our self), the letting go of any resentment, anger, dislike for some offense against us. Forgiveness or mercy is the law of God. Jesus prayed, "Forgive our debts as we have forgiven our debtors." When we are in a state of Being it is our own Inner Christ that forgives our own delinquencies. It is our own Inner Christ that forgives other's delinquencies. And it is based on love. It is not a "head" forgiveness but is a "heart" forgiveness. Both in balance bring true forgiveness or mercy.

As stated, I believe Jesus was speaking directly to the potential Mystic. Now the Mystic is not full blown perfect. The Mystic is on the Path, and the Goal is the Mystic Marriage. So with this Beatitude we have a most significant attitude for our progress. Take it seriously. It is a BE-ATTITUDE.

Forgiveness comes from the love of God, love of our Self, love of our neighbor, and love of so-called enemies, which include the Russians, the Iraqis, the Germans. In reply to the question, "Who is my neighbor?" Jesus answered by telling the parable of the Good Samaritan (Luke 10:25-37). Now the Samaritans were held in ill repute by the Jews who despised them. The Samaritans had the right to hate back. The Old Testament Law was, "If anyone injures his neighbor, whatever he has done must be done to him: fracture for fracture, eye for eye, tooth for tooth. As he has injured the other, so he is to be injured" (Lev. 24:19,20). But the Samaritan saw the need of a fellow human being, and he forgave the Israelite's hate for him and his brothers and sisters and had mercy for the robbed Israelite. This is forgiveness and mercy.

Mercy, compassion, love, all One. As a Mystic, Jesus gave that love and compassion in prayers, in giving, in healing, in teaching, in his Crucifixion and his Resurrection.

Compassion and mercy and love for the peoples of this earth make our forgiveness of them automatic.

"Great peace have they who love thy Law and nothing shall offend them" (Psalm 119:165 KJV).

That is mercy? That is mercy. Nothing shall offend them.

When you have reached a certain level of awareness of your Christ all thoughts will bear mercy. It is not our actions nor our words only that convey mercy. Our thoughts will also be centered in mercy and our feelings will come forth in our actions.

The thoughts of a Mystic are very powerful. They carry the energy of the Word. The Mystic has much responsibility for the welfare of the people near and far. Oneness with the Universal Energy carries the weight of God-thought. The Mystic knows this, and the thoughts are clear and positive for the welfare of the world. And forgiveness will be automatic. In fact, "nothing shall offend thee."

6. Blessed are the pure in heart for they will see God.
(Matthew 5:8)

Who are the pure in Heart? What does the heart symbolize? What is purity? And to "see God," does that mean we will see God with our physical eyes? All of this needs symbolic interpretation.

The heart has had so many interpretations that it behooves us to choose one that fits our Be-Attitude. The heart is the center of our physical life essence. When clogged, the heart does

65

not pump our blood to the rest of the body. It must have purity.

The heart can symbolize love. It can symbolize the feeling nature. The heart, to be pure, needs special attention. Let us use love from the heart to indicate the "pure in heart."

The pure in heart, the Mystic's heart, filled with love, brings God closer. Seeing God is being at One with God. The high ecstasy experience of Oneness in love is "seeing God." We do not have to die to "see" God. But we do need to live a pure life to see God else our "eyes" may be veiled. We see God in others also, if we look for It. Many are showing God to us but sometimes we are blind to that Essence in another. Pureness of heart is life to those on the Path.

Everything Jesus did was based on pure love. Thus it should be for the Mystic. Pure love can only bring a high moral sense, not based on what society or church teaches, but an Inner Knowing of what is right for our neighbor and for our self.

Purity, sacrifice of outer attachments and desires, our service to others, all result from pureness of heart. Being at One with Spirit we see Spirit. No one else can show us how. It is an Inside Job.

7. Blessed are the peacemakers, for they will be called children of God. (Matthew 5:9 KJV)

Isn't peace a primary goal for mankind in general? I do not mean world peace. I mean peace of mind, peace within, a peaceful heart, a body at peace. For the Mystic, peace naturally follows as one goes often to the Silence within, to the peace within. Within one's consciousness is the well for our peace. Peace is harmony of body, soul, mind and emotions. And Peace is based on love. It all comes back to love.

So the peacemakers start first with themselves. Peace in the outer flows as the Mystic is peaceful within. Nothing can disturb that Inner Peace. No lack, no hurt, no seeming illness disturbs that peace. It is the Way of a God-centered life.

Again, "Great peace have they who love thy law, and nothing shall offend them" (Psalms 119:165 KJV).

The author of peace is the Almighty according to Emma Curtis Hopkins. It is keeping our attention on the High Watch that brings peace and harmony into our lives.

Peace comes to us through confidence in God's Goodness and in our Self to handle any challenge on the Mystic Path. Oh, for the moment our old habit may disturb us but turning within to the Author of Peace, the Christ, will bring peace without mind-understanding, without left brain understanding. Real peace does not lie in logic and reasoning but in the Silence of God, in the Love of the heart.

Harmony is peace. Living in harmony with our Self and our neighbors is an act of pure love. We love our neighbors, we see the Good that lies behind their mistakes and know all is in Divine Order. We all learn from our mistakes.

Fear is probably the greatest disturber of peace. Fear is so much of the human condition. But for the Mystic all fear is lost in faith, in knowing, in Being-With-Being, Being-With-Being in the Silence. Being-With-Being is being there for those who are hurting, for those who are sick, for those who need a helping hand. For Being is God and God uses us to heal the helpless and the hurting to wellness and peace.

Peaceful living is serving others in peace without allowing the seeming disorder to intrude upon that peace. Service, a must for the Mystic, is given in peace and in pure confidence that all is well.

And to be a Child of God is of course exemplified best in the life and teachings of Jesus Christ. To rise to the pure heights of Elysian fields and know God is to be a Child of God. Jesus was not the only Son of God. He said we could all be Children of God if we are peacemakers.

Our consciousness of peace, our acts of peace, our awareness of the need for peace in the lives of others and our service to peace makes us peacemakers. Then peace will come on earth between all nations, all individuals. For peace begins in the heart of each person and peace must come or destruction follows.

Jesus knew the propensity of human beings to be competitive, to want to be the strongest and have the greatest nation. But he knew that peace would not reign until the people on earth realized the greatness of peace. It is as true today as it was 2000 years ago. The Mystic has lost all competitiveness and is cooperating with the God of Peace in thought, word, and deed. And the Mystic affects the rest of the world.

8. Blessed are those who are persecuted because of righteousness for theirs is the kingdom of Heaven.
(Matthew 5:10)

Previously I have defined righteousness as right-use-ness of our God inspired gifts. Righteousness in the ultimate is Oneness with God. That is the most righteous.

As we go on our Path becoming ever more aware of our Divinity, following the Inner Guidance, we may feel we are being persecuted. That persecution may not come from others in our life, but we may feel persecuted by life experiences.

"I never promised you a rose garden" may often be remembered as an explanation for the cleansing that goes on in our unconscious, in our conscious mind, in our personal affairs. We may have sickness of body or emotions. We may lose financially. We may lose a dear one. These may happen as a result of our choosing the Path to Oneness. Do not despair. The rose garden will come again. The Path of righteousness will lead us on.

All of this is necessary because a major change in our life will naturally follow such a major change in our thinking. All is balanced, and often we just have to stand and wait, being sure that the Goodness of God is handling these seeming persecutions. More of these persecutions may happen at the beginning of our Journey but they may happen all along the Way. Stand steady! The Kingdom of Heaven awaits.

At these times when peace seems to have fled one should continue to "Look Up" to the One, to call on the name of Jesus Christ, and to wait.

Persecution for righteousness' sake may also come from others. Choosing the Mystic Path puts one on a track that seems strange to others in our life. Giving up relationships, letting go of the need for many things, seeing the Good in all, enjoying solitude—all of these may seem strange to the average world-centered person. And they may persecute us out of their own fear, out of their own Shadow.

Jesus said, "Blessed are those who are persecuted for righteousness (centered in God)." How could we be blessed by persecution?

We are blessed for we need challenges in order to become strong in our Faith. The Mystic is Being-With-Being. When the world impinges on the Path then one digs deeper, lets go and lets God. As God heals us, then we rise to greater heights or depths of our Being. Challenges are necessary to test us, to let us look at ourselves, to decide what needs improvement or what needs eradication to clear our view of God, in order to "Look Up" clearly. And the greater our challenges, our persecutions, the greater the test of our Faith, of our choice of Being.

Jesus is our greatest example, of course. Throughout the persecutions experienced during his ministry and especially the last days of his life on earth, he held steady. Only once or twice did he seem to waver. But he continued on his Path and the Kingdom of Heaven became a Reality for him.

The Kingdom of Heaven is what Jesus promised us. It is reaching that high level of Being One with the God of All. It is Enlightenment, it is Nirvana, it is Cosmic Consciousness, it is the Mystical Marriage. It is our Aim. That is our Goal. And Jesus says that being persecuted for Righteousness, for the Goal, will bring us to Oneness.

Thus ends the Eight Beatitudes. The next one is really a reiteration of the eighth one. These Eight are reminiscent of the Eight Fold Path of the Buddha's teaching. They are a wonderful guide no matter the level of the Aspirant. The teaching for the aspiring Mystic is there and we would do well as Seekers on the Path to study them over and over and make them a part of our Guidance.

Now let us finish the Mystic Jesus' teaching.

> Blessed are you when people insult you, persecute you and falsely say all kinds of evil against you because of me. Rejoice and be glad because great is your reward in heaven, for in the same way they persecuted the prophets who came before you. (Matthew 5:11, 12)

Heaven is not out there but is here—it is the inner life of God. It is the Silence, it is Internal Peace, it is rest to the soul, it is comfort for the mind, and the heart. It is here and now.

We can endure all things for the great reward of knowing this Inner Peace. When we are persecuted we will have our greatest opportunity to experience Unconditional Love, the Love that Jesus Christ exemplified. And the expression of this Love is what we are here for. These persecutions can be seen

69

as a blessing as we meet them with deeper, more Christ-like Love.

Complaining is out. We are not here to satisfy our earth longings but our spiritual longings.

It has been our choice. Our Soul has guided us to this Path. If we are misunderstood we will know why. The choice of expressing our talent may not be what another would have chosen for us. Our creativity that comes from this Inner Voice may be, and usually is, different from any other than has been written, or invented, or painted, or sung. But it is right for us.

The power of the Master is with the Mystic. The Presence of the Master is with the Mystic. "And surely I will be with you always to the very end of the age" (Matthew 28:20b). The Christ is speaking.

We live according to the commands from our Christ and are unafraid. We have overcome that universal human bondage of fear. We have no fear for we are in the presence of all That Is. We are free—truly free. And so the persecution amounts to nothing.

We are making the right choices for our individual life and we rejoice for the Kingdom of Heaven is our goal, and we are It.

At some point on our Mystic Path there will be no more suffering, no more persecutions. Oh, I know that the traditional Christian theology points out that Jesus suffered for our sins. But I do not believe he suffered. He was above suffering. He was One with God, and does God suffer? Suffering is a human characteristic. How can God suffer? God is all Good. And so we of the metaphysical/mystical philosophy know that if we expect persecution, if we allow the criticism of others to shake us out of our peace, if we believe that suffering is our lot— then so be it. It will come to us. We can, at some point on the Mystic Journey, rise above being persecuted or at least being affected by persecution. That is the Path in God.

The Mystic Path gets easier as we become more and more Centered in Unconditional Love. Then "Great peace have they which love thy law" becomes true for us.

Peace, love, law, no offense. That is where we are as aspiring Mystics. We are in our rightful place and His right-use-ness is our theme.

These Beatitudes as interpreted for our Mystical Journey have the blessing of Jesus Christ. He taught them to the Disciples, and these inspired men and women went their way rejoicing when they realized their Bliss in teaching and imparting to others the great teachings of Jesus Christ. We can do likewise.

PART II

Chapter 4

RESULTS OF THE MYSTIC PATH

Inherent in much of what we have previously written are the results of the Mystic Path. It is clear that life has taken on a different hue. It is clear that one cannot go back again. It is clear that the life of the Mystic is not an ordinary one but one of great devotion, one of Union, one of Loving and Being that which has been described as the Highest.

But in the interest of practicality, for the Mystic is practical, which is basically Divine, we shall discuss the Way of the Mystic after Union of the Soul with God. As long as the Soul inhabits a physical body which walks on earth, so long are practical applications of this Divine Ineffable experience needed.

Much of what follows has been gleaned from the written accounts of great Mystics, either their account or that of a follower or admirer. Also will be included my own experience, for although Perfection has not been achieved in my life, I feel my life illustrates some of these high achievements, however lacking they may be in Ultimate Perfection.

Living the Mystic Path does not require one to follow an outer authority or code or creed. Living the Mystical Path is following completely directions from our own Inner Voice. It is surrender. It is making decisions in, it is choosing direction by, it is opening one's self to, that One Self. It is not for the faint hearted, and the courage and power one needs is forthcoming. Implementation of that all-pervasive Power is a must.

Being at One with the Mighty God is a major goal of all of humankind, consciously or unconsciously. Those who see another Mystic as being their Guide and their Guru may get nowhere. The Inner Guru is the one the aspiring Mystic follows. The genuine Mystic would in all humility discourage any Pilgrim from following his Way. Jesus said "Follow me" but he was not referring to the person Jesus but the Christ, the Holy Spirit which he exemplified in all of his words and acts. Each one of us, each Soul, has its own unique Path. Any instruction from another, whether a physical guide or Spirit guide, should be tested by one's Inner Christ. The Mystic is humble and only gives description of their own Path. This may be helpful but does not decree the Path for another.

The Mystic who has reached an experience of the Unitive Marriage is humble. The ego has been transformed into the realization that "I of myself can do nothing" (John 5:30 KJV). "The Father within me doeth the work." Jesus, our greatest example, was speaking. But Jesus did not encourage his followers to relive his life. He guided them to their Inner Counselor, the Christ, for their life Path. He was humble for he knew that all comes from the Father of Light.

When we speak of the Mystical Marriage we are not speaking of a once only experience. The Mystic may have such an experience many times, but each one takes them deeper or higher. The Unitive Life, as Evelyn Underhill calls it, may need re-experiencing over and over. The rapture experience of pure ecstasy and love that comes to the Mystic in high moments or even in dreams is an experience of Union, or a holy Christ-like experience. And this consummation of the Marriage is the Joy and Privilege of the Mystical Way.

Mystics may have disturbances in their life. The Kingdom of Heaven is at hand, but Mystics are still in physical earth living, and this may make them subject to earth demands. However, this becomes less and less often. The desires of the flesh experiences are transformed into the guidance, this in-filling, of the Spirit.

Mystics take care of their needs for food and rest—a must. The physical and mental bodies require it. Mystics take care of those who are dependent on them for love, cherishing, physical and emotional needs fulfillment. Mystics do not shirk their duties. However, Mystics do not allow these responsibilities to interfere with the Centeredness on the Path. Mystics do not allow those near to them to usurp their freedom to be as the

Christ directs them to be. If there are those who are too dependent, the Mystic may need to break free from them.

The Mystic is a giver and as Christ's and God's representative on earth continues to give to others. This is a demonstration of Unqualified Love.

Even though one has responsibilities to fulfill to another the Mystic is unattached. Detachment means that one is not dependent on another for the food of emotional good that one needs. All attachment is to God whereby the Inflow of love, wisdom, joy, creativity meets the needs of the Mystic which were fulfilled by people in their life in the past. Loving unconditionally requires detachment.

Mystics are Joy-filled. Filled with laughter and light heartedness. Child play, skipping and dancing, joy of life expresses and flows from them constantly. This may not be understood by others who believe the religionist should be solemn and sad. Often in church ritual the sorrow of the Crucifixion is reenacted. But the Mystic knows the Joy of nature, of the stars, of the bubbling brook and also the peacefulness of the deep flowing river. That peace is full of joy, laughter, joking, seeing the ridiculous. These are the mark of the true Mystic. The solemnity of the death of Jesus is raised to the realization of the Resurrection. That is celebrated in their life, also.

Mystics have no fear of death. In fact, many believe that their physical body will have no death but will be transformed into pure Light and find another dimension of expression. We know this is possible. This mystical experience of seeing a Light Being in the form of a human body, impregnated by Pure Light, appearing to the physical eyes of many, proves this. Even those who believe that eventually the physical body will drop know that there is only Life. The Soul is ever alive, and when Mystics have wholeness, they are filled with Light and Life.

And of course, as stated many times before, the Mystic is fulfilled by being of service to humanity and God. The Mystic cannot help but serve. One is so filled with the Essence that one would "burst" if there were no outlet.

The Eastern Mystic often expresses this service through separation from active involvement with others, withdraws to the forest or cave, lets go of all thought that hinders, and lives peacefully meditating and praying, lifting the vibrations of humankind which affect the well-being of all.

The Western Mystic has periods of tranquility, of separation from the world, of meditation and connection with Divinity and then goes into the world in the activity of service. For some this service may be meditation and prayer, but most Western Mystics are active in lifting the burdens of ignorance of humankind. Serving the needs of others through many activities, teaching, writing, art work, mundane physical work—all and many other forms of service are participated in. The Creativity of the soul of the Mystic must find expression for the tranquility of the soul to be undisturbed. Giving out the love that inflows is most rewarding, not in the ego sense, but through a deep devotion to One Master and Teacher.

Service in the healing arts is a Path chosen by many. This can include service as a medical doctor, a nurse, a Shaman and all that lies between. Many new and old methods of healing are used by the creative Mystic as expression is given to healing others both mentally and physically.

Everyone has some gift to offer to those on earth and to offer on the alter of the Heart of God, which is the individual Soul. Creating something, bringing forth Wisdom, expressing a new discovery, developing a therapy that alleviates pain, inventing something that frees humankind from hard labor so more time and energy can be used to uplift consciousness—all of these and more come from God, from the Creative Principle. And we don't always plan to use or even recognize our gift. This was certainly true of me.

In my own life, the commission to write an interpretation of the Book of Revelation, my first book, came to me. I did not seek it. It was a gift from the Creative spirit to me and to the world as that book, *Revelation for a New Age*, goes forth to lift the consciousness of many. I only supplied the tools and the inner listening ear to carry out the creative act. Thus it can be with the Mystic. In fact, creativity will be. It cannot be avoided if one is committed to Oneness.

The Mystic must choose to be alone with the Lord for a long measure of time. Indeed it is not a choice after one experiences the Mystic Marriage, the Union with God. The Unitive Life requires isolation from others and the world's affairs. The daily news, the frivolous TV shows, the talk shows which deal with the negative, the sordid, the sick humor, the titillating remarks and sexual behavior which is not based on real love which are presented on TV and the movies—all of these need to be shirked. Any of the negative ways of the world brings down the Consciousness of the observer. The negativity of earth living will be passed by. Interest in these negative aspects of the world will be shunned automatically when the Mystic is devoted to God. The choice to be alone, in deep meditation, listening to the song of the heart and the love and guidance of the Inner Spirit will fill the needs of the Mystic and do much to lift the Consciousness of the world.

Lots of social activity will naturally pass away. Watching a sports match might be uplifting as the skill and devotion of the players are observed. But primarily it is God's work, God's recreation in which one is interested.

There will, of course, be recreational times, but the Mystic chooses those activities that are not in opposition to the Sacredness of God's Guidance. It is God's directed work, play, activities of seeing, hearing, touching that the Mystic enjoys.

And it is not lonely, this isolation. It is filled with so much interest in expanding one's knowledge by reading, listening to music that uplifts and heals, being involved in friendships that satisfy the need for human association that one cannot be lonely because the Mystic knows the Presence Within. "Yet I am not alone for my Father is with me." The Master Jesus Christ was speaking. (John 16:32)

One is never alone but may feel in need of human company at times. And of course meditation during times alone brings the richest blessings. Meditation for hours or even all night, as Jesus did, will bring richest rewards.

As to celibacy—that is an individual choice. Those who have the experience of the Mystic Marriage may choose not to have a sexual partner. In fact, most Mystics who have made their mark on the Consciousness of humankind have not been married or in a sexual relationship with another person. However, I hasten to add that living with a partner who is also on the Path can be very conducive to our own spiritual life. It depends on the person.

Many Eastern religions teach that celibacy is the better choice so that one can conserve the Life Energy that may be lost in the sexual act, to lift the physical body to a higher vibration of Pure Light and the spiritual Consciousness to a higher level. Some New Thought teachers in America taught the Path to regeneration over generation. (See *Twelve Powers of Man* by Charles Fillmore.) One will find the Truth for one's self as they follow their Guidance.

Overcoming the duality of earth living will come easily for the Mystic who has reached the Goal. The Goal is reached when one has become androgynous, has balanced the masculine and feminine, the active and the receptive, within the psyche. The feeling nature (feminine) and the masculine (intellect) have blended into Oneness. Perhaps this is the real Mystical Marriage. It is all within. The ecstasy of Inner co-habiting is limitless.

And love!! That is what it is all about. Again we do not have the words to explain it but the Mystic knows about love. It is innate—this knowledge of Love. It is the Father/Mother, the Christ, the Holy Spirit. It is experiencing that Love that the Mystical Marriage is all about. The ecstasy and joyfulness of the experience of Oneness is the epitome of Love. And the outflowing of that Love to others is the service that the Mystic expresses. I shall not enlarge upon Love. You know.

When one has reached the Mystic Marriage one has nothing for which to forgive another. There will be no more feelings of resentment, of anger, of hurt feelings. "Nothing shall offend them" (Psalms 119:165). Until that point is reached forgiveness of anyone who offends is needed, not so much for the person we forgive but for our own cleansing so that the Light of God can shine through to Consciousness. Old offenses must also be forgiven and ofttimes to learn what they are, we may need some deeper psychological probing by a spiritual, loving professional.

And Song!! Singing, music of the Spheres, which our great composers have captured in song, instrument and dance. What a lovely experience and even if we do not hear the rock beat as a holy experience, to some it may be.

The chanting and singing of the Mystic brings into Consciousness the vibrations of the Heavenly host. It is all for the expression of that Holiness that is unconsciously ours. Music is a part of our Being. The Mystic hears that music in the heart, ofttimes when dreaming, and expresses it outwardly in many ways. The song has always been a part of our worship, and the Mystic is attuned to the finest.

The Mystic knows peace and quiet and the Silence. That Silence is deep. It is indescribable. Silence does not really describe it, but it is the best word we have. It is Silence within. It is Silence within Silence. And then bubbles up Joy. It is Joy that fills the entire body, mind and Soul. Such Joy! And the Silence returns. It is as if the Spirit had greeted one with the effervescence of feeling. It is poetry. It is music. It is "I love you" from the depths. It is Love!

And it is the deep realization, the deep KNOWING that God is All, that there is nothing that is not God, that brings the Mystic to fulfillment. All along the Path of the metaphysical and the mystical we have been grasping after this Truth. Finally the Mystic KNOWS without doubt that all is Good, all is God, that the Presence is All and we are that Presence. "I am God" then becomes The Truth and Home has been reached.

Jesus Christ called the Mystic goal the Kingdom of Heaven and told us that it spread all around the earth. He also said the Kingdom of Heaven is within you (Luke 17:20, 21). He, the greatest Mystic, has much to teach us.

Between the metaphysical philosophy and the Mystical Way are many commonalities. Let us go now to the last section which compares the two. You may find that you are more Mystical than you have realized.

PART III

Chapter 1

SOME THOUGHTS ON THE METAPHYSICAL AND MYSTICAL

As we have studied in depth these two philosophies we have found more similarities than differences. Although this is true we also realize that to move from one to the other may require the Seeker to make big changes in their life: to be adaptable to change; to turn from the outer to the Inner for choices in life; to be patient and not expect completion in a day; to accept one's Self as Who one really is; to base one's thinking on intuition; to live life from that Intuitive Guidance; and to find a way to serve humanity.

There are those people who are happy with the progress they have made following the metaphysical philosophy and do not want to go to the Mystical Way. Well and good! They have freedom of choice and are on the right Path. After all, there is no Time and Space in the Godhead and NOW all is impregnated with Spirit. The Past is gone, the Future is not yet here. So there is no hurry. Just Be in the presence NOW and let God direct your Path. When the time has come for another Leap on your Path, It will come.

However, for those who feel unfulfilled, this book (I hope) has given some guidance and some courage to undertake the Silent Intuitive Way. The blending of the two will be found to accelerate growth toward Wholeness.

There are those in the traditional Christian teaching who have found themselves open to Mysticism. I should hope that something written here would encourage them to undertake the Way. The metaphysical Path is not necessary, of course. We know of many in the religions of the world who have become Mystics without benefit of the metaphysical teaching, so named. There are many Paths to Wholeness. I would not want to leave the impression that there is only one.

For those who are on the metaphysical Path and are considering stepping on the mystical Path, I should like to draw to their attention again the similarities and differences in the two Paths. We have already pointed this out in other chapters but this one will go deeper as well as be more comprehensive. Taking a deep breath, "letting go" and Letting God will open one to the Mystic Way.

Many times we do not choose the Mystic Path. Many times it comes to us inadvertently. Whether we accept it is our choice; we are free.

And you do not have to be perfect to be chosen. Many who feel they are the least perfect find themselves guided to fulfill a great work. When the work is chosen for you, you only need to say "Yes Lord" and follow.

Once you have realized where you are on the Path you may find that the metaphysical teachings are helpful but may interrupt the Flow. This is especially true in the need to give up the idea that thought control is a first requirement to bring you Higher. After much meditation, your intuition, the Voice Within, will get your attention, and you will start living from There, and thinking from There.

Many serious students of the metaphysical way are into "head knowledge." They have studied, read, prayed, gone to classes, attended church and are chuck full of knowledge. But the Goal is Christ Consciousness. With "head knowledge," we are "out there" instead of "in here." All of those activities are merely a preparation for the Mystic Life and are important. But it is the conversion to the Ineffable Presence that will bring one that for which they yearn, Oneness.

Many of these Pilgrims may be blocked by past mistakes, past unforgiveness, selfish caring for themselves without giving to others. They may still be tied to the theology and creeds of the church they attended as a child. Perhaps it is too frightening a step to leave family and friends for a new direction to the Kingdom of Heaven. Maybe this describes where you are.

I believe that old tapes need to be cleared out if we are to find the full glory of the Mystic Path. Most of us are carrying old baggage in our unconscious that needs bringing to the surface and letting go. Our Shadow over our Good may need to be expunged or cleansed. All of us have a Shadow or two or three that is keeping our Good from us. To cleanse our unconscious may be part of our Path. I recommend Jungian analysis to help dream interpretation, or group work with a qualified leader, or attention to whatever comes up in meditation and dealing with it openly. The Spirit cannot shine through if there is too much darkness around our Soul Light.

Another block to the metaphysical student and Mystic is the idea that one can cover up the negative by thinking and speaking from the positive. This may work for some, but covering up *facts* that are keeping us from advancing on the Path will finally backfire. *Facts* need to be admitted and perhaps some action needs to be taken to deal with and to heal the negative or to leave it. The affirmations of Good will help but not admitting the *facts* of a situation may be your greatest block to wholeness. The student who steps on the Mystic Path may still need some cleansing.

Another block on the Path to Oneness for the student is focusing on bringing Good to your Path but giving no attention to the needs of others. What are love and compassion for? How can we truly seek Oneness with God if we are not loving and giving, not only to our family and friends, but to the deprived, the underprivileged, the sick, the despondent people of this world? Giving our love, that bubbles from the Center, to others is balance. And it is balance that we as human beings need. The Mystic life especially needs that. So many of the affirmations are for one's self, and one's loved ones when we are on the metaphysical level. Jesus gave to all—the beggar, the wealthy, the powerful. Should we do less? Not if we are interested in being a Mystic.

Humility, Jesus taught, is necessary for one entering the Kingdom of Heaven, and to stay there humility is a must. This does not mean that we call ourselves "worms of the dust," but we are really "heirs to God." But realizing that all comes from the Infinite One and that there is no limit to the expansion of our Consciousness of that One, will make us humble. This is a teaching for the metaphysician and the Mystic.

Most metaphysical teaching does not stress morality as it assumes that everyone is being guided by their Inner Christ and consciously living under the Law of Cause and Effect. Most of us having grown up in a Christian society know the "Thou shalt nots." However, the metaphysical classes and books, for the most part, do not lay down any guidance for morals, ethics, values except in a general sense. So where does one go for help?

On the Mystic Path, if you are deeply listening, *There* will be your guidance. For the Spirit of Truth, the Counselor has all Guidance. In the Mystic Way, your behavior will be in "sync" with either the teachings of Jesus, or the Buddha, or the Tao, etc. Go to the scripture of the world religions and find your answers. The Law of Cause and Effect will bring you reward or pain early on. You may have to learn your direction by trial and error.

Jesus' law is, "Do to others as you would have them do to you" (Luke 6:31). That requires us to be "wise as serpents and harmless as doves" (Matthew 10:16b KJV). This he said to his disciples as he gave them instructions for their missionary journey. Moral guidance lies within the scripture, also.

Basically I believe that morality is based on honesty and Truth. Now *what is Truth* has been argued for ages, and I would say that your Truth may be different from others. However, to be honest in all your thoughts, words, and actions can bring nothing else but moral living. And the greatest Law as taught by Jesus will be your basis, to wit, "Love the Lord your God with all your heart, soul, and mind and your neighbor as yourself." That Self is the large Self, not the small self.

Prayer and meditation are stressed in the metaphysical philosophy. Prayer, in my definition, is talking to God, asking, commanding, praising. Meditation is listening, going into the Silence. Prayer and meditation are combined on the Mystic Path. If you have had guided meditation in churches and classes you may be ready for silent meditation on your own. The silence is where the Spirit dwells and the Silence brings forth our greatest intuitive Knowings. This is the Mystic Way.

The metaphysical student reads many books. A large collection accrues in most homes. If you are progressing on the Path you will be reaching out to more difficult ones to understand. Read from the Mystics. Read books about Carl Jung's teaching and eventually read books he wrote. Read books of the great World Religions. Read books by Joseph Campbell. Read metaphysical interpretations of the Bible. Expand your intellect and your Consciousness by exposure to those who have written from a high level of Consciousness. Go beyond the writings for the metaphysical beginner. Be broad in exposure to mystical ideas. And you can be sure that the right books will come to you.

Throughout my Journey I have been guided by many great books written by or about metaphysicians and Mystics. Each time I was ready for a new expansion, the right book would almost "seek me out." The Spirit within knew my needs and guided me. Synchronistic occurrences, finding the right book, were God directed. Be open and receptive to that Guidance and you will be taught by the right person at the right time. Eventually more time will be spent in meditating, creating, serving than in reading. The need for outer reinforcement of what you already know will pass the further you go on your Path.

You may get to the point that church attendance is no longer as important to you as it once was. Many ministers in the metaphysical churches are still teaching from the pulpit to the beginner.

However, teaching in some classes may be more advanced and a group is most helpful when you need to share and ask questions. Starting your own group in your home and studying a book on mysticism may fill that need. You will attract the right ones to you for that endeavor. Group meditation is especially effective to raise personal and world Consciousness. Advance at your own rate from where you are. Let your Inner Guide direct you. Group worship is needed by many on the Path. Let your needs guide you.

You may want to continue to support the church or center by financial giving. You will certainly want to recommend church and class attendance to one who is beginning to recognize their spiritual need. Also, your Consciousness may be needed in that church or center and you will share It with others as you attend.

You may be fulfilling the need of the group by attending church services. Your Consciousness can lift the Consciousness of others attending. You may be called to be the Light to others in Churches, classes or other settings where groups meet.

Jesus said, "You are the light of the world" (Matthew 5:14a) and "Let your light shine before men, that they may see your good deeds and praise your Father in heaven" (Matthew 5:16). Your light may lift another to their Light. Also group attendance can balance the solitude in which you find yourself on the Mystic Path. Let your needs guide you and also give of your Consciousness to others where needed.

You may want to go more deeply into the metaphysical philosophy by studying to be a teacher, a counselor, a practitioner, or a minister. The service one performs in those areas is commendable and needed. If one is led to the Mystic life and can teach or preach of it inside the church organization, it will be a great service as more and more who are not fulfilled by traditional church teaching or metaphysical teaching are looking for a more expanded view of the Divine.

I have spoken of the Mystic's need to be of service to humankind. This is often not stressed in many metaphysical teachings, although many students are led to be of service without reliance on metaphysical teaching. The Spiritual Journey (The Hero's Heroine's Journey, as described by Joseph Campbell) necessitates each one finding their Bliss in creativity, in service, in living, in work. This Bliss, this feeling of Righteousness (Right-use-ness) may indicate that you have found what you came to do for humankind during this earth life. The Mystics know that each one of us has a responsibility to fulfill and each may find this in the work they perform. Being a homemaker, a parent, a provider may be Bliss for a time. One might realize that releasing these responsibilities may be necessary in order to take up some other form of service. This is especially true of those who step on the Mystic path. Inner Guidance often dictates the change.

Emma Curtis Hopkins mentions many qualities of the Mystic in her book *High Mysticism.* One is that when we are doing what we came to do, we will have effortless success. All work is inspired activity when we reach a certain level on our Mystic Path. It is invigorating, it is blissful, it is not depleting. Test your main activity against that criteria.

She also teaches that the Mystic will come to not only realize, but to KNOW, that all is Good. The Mystic sees through the eyes of love. "The Christ is in each person" comes forth to greet the Mystic. All is Good.

The metaphysical students are taught that one has control over their lives. They are taught that all that comes to them is due to their own thought processes. This often lays a guilt trip on them. When things go wrong in their life they believe they have done something or had a thought or imagining that brought on the disease, the disturbance, the problem. And this may be true at that level.

The difference between the metaphysician and the Mystic in this regard is that the person in the metaphysical philosophy is still taking cognitive responsibility for all that happens to them. Thought control, their responsibility, is taught. "What have I been thinking, doing, saying, believing that brought this on?" This is well and good at that level. We have to start somewhere.

The Mystic is more inclined to surrender the responsibility for the seeming negative occurrence, know that only Good can come from it, and wait for the Grace of God to come forth and show the Way. The Mystic does not lose faith in themself or in God. They wait for the teaching that will come forth from the experience that will lift them to a higher level of Consciousness.

Sometimes the Mystic expects perfection of themself. If the Dark Night comes on, they are prone to believe they are responsible, that somehow they have "let God down." What those Mystics who talk about the Dark Night say is that one must know that "This too shall pass" and with deep emotional and spiritual devotion stay on the path. Eventually the Light dawns and they see this time as another opportunity to go higher.

We must remember that when we go from one level of Consciousness to another we may have these difficult times. All that we have based our former Consciousness on, the foundation of it, has been moved, and the structure may tremble. But our new state will bring us more, much more. We just pray and wait.

In both, I think one important factor is being ignored—race or human consciousness, i.e., what the society around one believes and thinks. Living in a human society impresses our thinking. When that society has a particular way of addressing a problem, and we are exposed daily to that direction, we can pick up some very negative ideas that may interfere with our Mystical Way. Perhaps, like some Mystics, we should not listen to the modern media, or read the newspapers, and be free of influence by the race or human consciousness. I believe, however, that one should be able to live in human society, be aware of the race consciousness on the human plane and not be pulled down by it. We should rise to the high level of God Knowing, that all is Good and wait to see the Good that accrues from the seeming negative.

There are several other characteristics of the metaphysical Path that I should like to address for more mystical guidance. The differences of the two Paths have already been made apparent but the need to repeat some of these teachings will bring more understanding.

Freedom is truly ours when on the Mystical Path. Freedom from other's opinion, freedom from church dogma and creed, freedom from our own intellectual choices, freedom to Be who we really are. What a wonderful gift and one toward which all of humanity is striving. This Freedom is not based on lack of responsibility but on greater responsibility to Spiritual service to God and humanity. Freedom to be the Self carries a large price, sometimes, but our deepest desire is for peace and love through freedom. That is our Goal.

Mystics come from all religious persuasions and *no* religious persuasion. Each teaching is fulfilling the needs of the people engaged in that particular form of worship. Each has their own particular Teacher be it avatar, rishi, rebbi, or shaman. The Mystic in the Christian culture may turn to Jesus Christ as their Guide and Way. However, Jesus did not recommend blind following of his Way but a following of each one's Inner Spirit. Jesus Christ's teachings are of the highest and many Mystics devote their Way to this Greatest Mystic.

The use of intellect, visualizing, repetitious prayers and chants may not be the Way of the Christian Mystic. The Mystic depends completely on God's largesse. The metaphysical student may still need to visualize, to repeat affirmations over and over in order to affect changes in their own concept of what needs to be done for their Good. These exercises are not needed by the Mystic for all Good comes to them without effort. The Holiness of God's Love is made conscious.

It is hard to believe, after one has accepted that they are learning from the Law of Cause and Effect, that one can rise above that Law. The Mystic on their Path has also learned much from the Effect but now when a negative Effect comes they see it as an opportunity for learning and the Cause may not lie in their choices but in the Inevitable, Undiminishing Desire of God for the Mystic to rise higher. The Cause is God's Way of nudging the Mystic to a closer awareness. Effects are rungs on the ladder of Ascension.

Karma is wiped out in the true Love and Compassion of the Seeker on the Mystic Path. As one aims for completion all is forgiven, all is neutralized. All is understood and one does not need to repay debts to themself or others. Love fully practiced wipes the slate clean.

Some Mystics believe in Reincarnation; others see Heaven as potentially here and now and no need for Reincarnation faces them. No need to return to a physical body is believed. However, there are those who believe they may return in order to serve and help others become fully Enlightened. One on the Metaphysical Path may see Reincarnation as another chance to express and Be that Spirit which they know dimly that they are.

The Mystic is relaxed as far as needs for their physical living is concerned. It may be at mere subsistence level or it may be at a comfortable and luxurious level. Whatever God provides will be a gift and duly appreciated. The Mystic does not strive for more materialism. The Mystic relaxes and the bounty of the Universe falls into their lap. The Mystic's worship of God includes thanksgiving for all that is provided. The metaphysician may not yet fully realize the Bounty of His Love. The Mystic gives generously and receives generously. This, also, the metaphysician learns.

And what about relationships? How are they different?

The person centered in metaphysical living usually has many relationships with those who have no interest in that Path. These persons often live a split life, socially speaking, until they, little by little, give up attachment to those in their social or family circle who are slowing the pace of their adherence to the metaphysical philosophy. If they change over to the Mystic Way there may be many ripples and pains in relationships.

Little by little, or maybe suddenly, depending on the path of the Mystic, many relationships drop off. This is because the Mystic needs less social life, less contact with others and more solitude. Usually before one steps on the Mystic path many of these decisions have been made. The Mystic may be in a cloister, or monastery, or convent, or spiritual commune but everyone in these organized groups is not interested in mysticism. So even there, the Mystics withdraw more and more from the society of others.

Most, not all, do not choose to be a recluse for serving in the world brings them in contact with many. But more time apart from others, in solitude, usually becomes their Path. Their companions become those who are on a similar Search.

The Kingdom of Heaven state of Consciousness is the Mystic's Goal while for the metaphysician, a more peaceful, loving life satisfies them. The focus of their life will change as they get the vision of Wholeness so strongly in their awareness that they cannot avoid it. They will search in Jesus' teaching for Guidance; they will meditate for longer periods; they will practice that deep Silence and Knowing. They have stepped on the Mystic Path.

Like the metaphysician, no hell, devil or evil plague the Mystic's thoughts. They KNOW All is Good. They realize their need to express that Good in all their thoughts, words and undertakings. And at first there are many ups and downs but eventually as they depend more and more on their Intuitive Knowing to feed their intellect, they will advance rapidly on their Path.

Balance in all things and relationships; masculine and feminine within the psyche; human and divine; become Reality for the Mystic. Work and play, meditation and activity, the Silence and the speech—all become balanced in the Mystic's life.

How expansive the metaphysical teachings are. It is for those who are discontented, have had a mistaken interpretation of who they are and have not found religious teachings that fit their Inner Knowing. How beautifully the metaphysical way fills their needs! And then to move to the Mystic—how Divine!

Both Paths are wonderful. I know from experience. How soul enriching it was when I found the metaphysical philosophy and learned I was not alone in my Search for God! Also when, I as a woman, realized that God's Love for me was not dependent on what sex I was but on my allegiance to that Inner Spirit, I was well on the Way to the Mystic Path.

Before we conclude, let us review the Seven Mansions of St.Teresa of Avila from her *Interior Castle* which can give the Seeker some measure of what they are on the Path.

It is all One, the metaphysical and the Mystical. When we see them thusly we are on our Way to *that* Oneness of Being.

PART III

Chapter 2

TERESA OF AVILA'S *INTERIOR CASTLE*

Let us close by exploring the teaching of St. Teresa of Avila on the Seven Mansions in her book *Interior Castle*. They blend the metaphysical and the mystical paths.

The first Six Mansions she describes are our experiences on the Path to the King. The Seventh Mansion is the center of the Castle where the King abides and where we become One.

The *First Mansion* is outside the Castle in the courtyard. It contains venomous creatures. These are the human/earthly desires that partially satisfy our longing and partly make us restless. They tempt us to quiet our greatest desire, Oneness with God. The warmth of the Spirit is faint, still God is there.

The *Second Mansion* is the place of timid turning to God. It is called "Practice and Prayer." Here the person, the soul, is beginning to find some peace in sermons, reading uplifting books, classes, association with like-minded people. There are still attacks on their peace. Their first spiritual feeling may come to them, an opening of Truth.

The *Third Mansion*, the "Mansion of Exemplary Life," is where the Pilgrim is living a good life led by thought control, by denials and affirmations, performing acts of charity, and loving their neighbor. Life is in pretty good order and one may choose to go no further into the Castle.

The *Fourth Mansion* is called "Prayer and Quiet." This is the first entering into Consciousness of the supernatural elements of the mystical life. God's Guidance becomes more and more a way of life. Meditation will be a must as one listens to the Inner Voice.

The *Fifth Mansion*, called the "Spiritual Betrothal of Prayer of Union," is the place of deep contemplating, experiencing the Silence. It is a deeper level of awareness of God. Ecstasy and Joy are a part of the Inner experience. Here one touches the Essence, does not understand it with the intellect, and cannot describe it. However, there may still be suffering, for the Victory has not yet been won.

The *Sixth Mansion* is so close to the Center Mansion that one may believe that nothing, no suffering, can interrupt. This mansion is called "The Dark Night of the Soul." Here one may have their greatest challenge. It is like a test to the Mystic before going to the Heights or the most Central Spiritual experience. Overcoming this challenge will give the Pilgrim their greatest teaching. (Some Mystics do not think this step is necessary for full Enlightenment. Teresa, being of the Catholic philosophy and believing that each must suffer as Jesus suffered, may be expecting the suffering, and so it comes. Those who do not believe that suffering is necessary may not have this Dark Night experience.)

The *Seventh Mansion* is called the "Spiritual Marriage." Here dwells the King, it may be called the Kingdom of Heaven. Here the Soul and God become One. There is complete transformation, peace without understanding, Pure Spiritual experience. This is true Enlightenment.

And so ends our adventure into examining the metaphysical philosophy and the Mystical Way, their similarities and differences. Which one we choose is up to our Souls' need to express in this lifetime. The Way will unfold for each of us in its own time. When we decide to surrender to God's Will completely we will have started another level of our Soul's Journey. We are each free to choose our Way. It is all One Path. So be it.

Epilogue

WHAT LIES
BEYOND MYSTICISM?

This is an Infinite Path, this developing a relationship to the Highest that humankind has been unable to fully understand. Our changing realization of what this Universal Energy is has evolved over the ages. Much of our realization of its meaning has resulted from the culture and the religion that was dominant in our experience. Now we are being pulled beyond that culture and religion to a planetary concept of Reality. And the walls will come tumbling down between the different cultures and religions as our Realization evolves.

We are witnessing today those walls being demolished. The Ecology movement has taken planetary dimensions. We are realizing that what is happening in the atmosphere in the United States is affecting the atmosphere in Europe. The tragedy of nuclear accidents is a case in point. We are beginning to awaken to the understanding that we are One on this round ball, and that we had better cooperate or we will demolish ourselves and it. We are indeed our brother's keeper!

There are those who have been termed Mystics who are special emissaries to our planet and have Truth that goes beyond the physical, emotional, intellectual worlds of our present realization. To recognize them, to listen to them, and to change our choices in terms of their spiritual leadership may be the next step. The Mystic then can be the leader of the planetary change.

On the Inner awareness, however, the leadership is lying dormant in many. The coming of the Cosmic Christ has already occurred, according to Matthew Fox, and is the catalyst that causes the changes. Being led by the Inner Spirit is a growing movement throughout the world. *There* is our next leader, and since the Christ is the same in each, the movement will have great power.

Yes, there is more, but if each of us raises our consciousness to the Christ Consciousness (or use another title from other religious persuasions that you wish), then a quantum leap shall have been taken. Let us each move toward the Christogenesis stage of Pierre Teilhard de Chardin as we join the Pilgrims on the Mystic Path. We shall then be ready for the next great leap of conscious realization of God either in this life or another. The Path has no ending. We can best serve as we understand where we are and then pursue the next level of Consciousness.

The basis for so many choices by humankind on this planet is on the intellectual, scientific level. To move from that to the ever expanding Reality of the Spirit will bring us higher in our understanding of *Who* is the world. And then infinity opens and we are on our Way.

GLOSSARY OF TERMS

ANIMA: The feminine element within a man's psyche. (See Jung's Psychology.)

ANIMUS: The masculine element within a woman's psyche. (See Jung's Psychology.)

CONSCIOUSNESS: Conscious awareness of God, of the Spirit.

CONTEMPLATION: A deep feeling of ecstasy, exceeding joy, sometimes a deep Silence that can result from meditation.

COSMIC CHRIST: The true Self or the inner Spirit, God with us, the likeness and image of God.

KUNDALINI: An Eastern word for Divine Energy. The serpent fire of regeneration lying at the base of the spine. The spine is the path up which it travels to regenerate the physical body, to change the physical to Light, or spiritual essence.

MEDITATION: A stopping of the thoughts by focusing on the one thought, one thing, on the breath, on a mantra. A touching of the inner Divinity in the Silence.

METAPHYSICAL: The knowledge which is beyond, which transcends the physical; a study of the science of Being; beyond physical laws.

MYSTIC: One who centers his/her life on knowledge and activity of the Spirit. The Mystic follows Guidance from the Invisible Presence.

NIRVANA: The extinction of the not-self (the ego) in the completion of the Self. It may be compared to the Kingdom of Heaven. A purely mystical conception.

OMEGA POINT: When all souls have become One with The Soul.

self (small "s"): The ego; the human self often egotistical; belief in self-will.

SELF (capital "S"): The Inner Divine Presence of the soul. The Christ.

SHADOW: That which is the unconscious or dark side of our personality which we do not consciously show to others and to our self, often a characteristic projected on others; that which covers the Soul consciousness.

BIBLIOGRAPHY

Aquarian Gospel of Jesus the Christ. Transcribed from Akashic Records by Levi. Marina del Rey, CA: DeVorss Publishing, 1969.

Braden, Charles. *Spirits in Rebellion, The Rise and Development of New Thought.* Dallas: Southern Methodist University Press, 1963.

Bucke, Richard Maurice, M.D. *Cosmic Consciousness.* New York: E.P.Dutton, 1969.

Cady, H. Emilie. *Lessons in Truth.* Unity Village, MO: Unity Books, 1884 (Text for Unity).

Campbell, Joseph. *The Power of Myth.* New York: Doubleday, 1988 (With Bill Moyers).

Capps, Walter Holden and Wendy M. Wright. *Silent Fire.* San Francisco: Harper & Row, 1978.

Divine Science, Its Principle and Practice. Compiled by committee from writings of Fannie B. James and Malinda E. Cramer. Denver Divine Science Federation International, 1957. (Text of Divine Science)

Eddy, Mary Baker. *Science and Health with Key to the Scriptures, Authorized Edition.* Christian Publishing Society, 1906.

Elder, Dorothy. *Revelation: For a New Age* (The Book of Revelation). Marina del Rey, Ca: DeVorss Publishing, 1981.

——————. *Women of the Bible Speak to Women of Today.* Marina del Rey, CA: DeVorss Publishing, 1986.

——————. *The Song of Songs and Enlightenment.* Marina del Rey, CA: DeVorss Publishing, 1988.

——————. *Isaiah, The Metaphysician.* (Unpublished)

Fillmore, Charles. *The Twelve Powers of Man.* Unity Village, MO: Unity School of Christianity, 1934.

Fox, Emmet. *Sermon on the Mount.* New York: Harper & Brothers, 1938.

Fox, Matthew. *The Coming of the Cosmic Christ.* San Francisco: Harper & Row, 1988.

Happold, F.C. *Mysticism: A Study and Anthology.* New York: Viking Penguin, 1963.

Heline, Corinne. *New Age Bible Interpretation* (7 Vols.). Los Angeles, CA: New Age Press, 1935-1954.

Holmes, Ernest. *The Science of Mind.* New York: Dodd, Mead & Company, 1938. (Text for Religious Science/Science of Mind)

Hopkins, Emma Curtis. *Scientific Christian Mental Practice.* Marina del Rey, CA: DeVorss & Co.

──────. *High Mysticism.* Marina del Rey, CA: DeVorss & Co., 1974.

James, William. *The Varieties of Religious Experience.* New York: Random House, 1929.

John of the Cross. *The Dark Night of the Soul.* Garden City, NY: Image Books, 1959.

Jung, Carl. *Memories, Dreams, Reflections.* New York: Vintage House, 1963.

Krishna, Gopi. *Kundalini: The Evolutionary Energy.* Boston: Shambhala, 1970.

Lamsa, George M. *The New Testament.* Philadelphia: A.J. Holman Company, 1933.

Metaphysical Bible Dictionary. Writings of Charles Fillmore. Unity Village, MO: Unity School of Christianity, 1931.

Noss, John B. *Man's Religions.* New York: MacMillan Co., 1974.

Parmahansa Yogananda. *Autobiography of a Yogi.* Los Angeles, CA: Self Realization Fellowship, 1969.

Peale, Norman Vincent. *The Power of Positive Thinking.* New York: Prentice-Hall, 1952.

Ramakrishna Vedanta Center. *Women Saints, East & West.* Hollywood, CA: Vedanta Press, 1979.

Sinetar, Marsha. *Ordinary People as Monks and Mystics.* New York: Paulist Press, 1986.

Teresa of Avila. *Interior Castle.* Garden City, NY: Doubleday, 1961.

──────. *The Way of Perfection.* Garden City, NY: Image Books, Doubleday & Co., 1964.

Teilhard de Chardin, Pierre. *The Phenomenon of Man.* New York: Harper & Row, 1965.

Underhill, Evelyn. *Mysticism.* Cleveland, OH: World Publishing Co., 1967.

VanDusen, Wilson. *The Presence of Other Worlds, The Psychology/ Spiritual Findings of Emanuel Swedenborg.* New York: Swedenborg Foundation, Third Printing, 1985.

White, John (Ed.). *What Is Enlightenment? Exploring the Call of the Spiritual Path.* Los Angeles, CA: Jeremy P. Tarcher, 1984.

Bible References:

KJV is King James Version
RSV is Revised Standard Version

ACKNOWLEDGMENTS

Excerpts reprinted by permission from:

What Is Enlightenment? by John White, copyright 1984 by John White. Reprinted by permission of John White and Jeremy P. Tarcher, Inc.

Memories, Dreams, Reflections, by Carl Jung, recorded and edited by Aniela Jaffé, translated from the German by Richard and Clara Winston, 1963. Reprinted by permission of Random House, Inc. Alfred A. Knopf, Inc.

Man's Religions, by John Noss, copyright 1984 by MacMillan Publishing Company.

ORDER FORM

YES, I want to invest $8.95 in a book that can open my Spiritual Journey to me. Please send _____ copies to:

Name _____Phone (_____) _____

Address _____

City _____State _____Zip _____

Here is my check for $_____

Make check payable to Doriel Publishing.

I have included $2 for postage for each copy and 3.8% state sales tax since I live in Colorado.

QUANTITY ORDERS INVITED

For bulk discount rates please call (303) 986-4711